HOW TO DAY TRADE FOR A LIVING

The Ultimate Beginner's Guide to Day Trading with Practical Steps

A.A Kaitlyn

CONTENTS

Part one: A Must Know

Part Two: A Must Do

Part one: A Must Know

Introduction to Day Trading

Day trading is a popular approach to trading in financial markets that involves buying and selling securities within a single trading day. Unlike long-term investing, day traders aim to profit from short-term price fluctuations. It is a fast-paced and dynamic activity that requires knowledge, skill, and discipline.

In day trading, traders utilize various strategies and techniques to identify opportunities and make quick trading decisions. They often rely on technical analysis, studying charts and indicators to predict price movements. Some traders also pay attention to market news and economic events that can impact the securities they trade.

The primary advantage of day trading is the potential for quick profits. Since positions are typically closed by the end of the day, day traders avoid overnight risks and can capitalize on intraday price volatility. However, it's important to note that day trading also carries risks, including the potential for significant losses.

To get started with day trading, you'll need a brokerage account that provides access to the markets you want to trade in. It's crucial to choose a reliable and regulated broker with competitive fees and a user-friendly trading platform. Additionally, having a fast internet connection and a reliable computer or laptop is essential for executing trades swiftly.

Successful day trading requires more than just a basic understanding of the markets. Traders need to develop and refine their trading strategies, which include entry and exit rules, risk management techniques, and profit targets. They also need to exercise emotional discipline to avoid impulsive decisions driven by fear or greed.

Continuous learning is a vital aspect of day trading. Markets evolve, and staying updated with market news, economic indicators, and industry trends is crucial for making informed trading decisions. Engaging in educational resources, such as books, online courses, and webinars, can help traders expand their knowledge and refine their skills.

While day trading can be financially rewarding, it is important to approach it with realistic expectations. Building expertise and consistently profitable results takes time and practice. It is advisable to start with a small trading capital and gradually increase it as you gain experience and confidence.

Day trading offers the potential for short-term profits by taking advantage of intraday price movements in financial markets. However, it requires dedication, continuous learning, and disciplined decision-making. If you are willing to put in the effort to learn and develop your skills, day trading can be an exciting and potentially lucrative endeavor.

Chapter one

Understanding Day Trading

1.1 What is Day Trading?

Day trading is a fast-paced trading approach where individuals buy and sell financial instruments within the same trading day. Unlike traditional investors who hold positions for longer periods, day traders aim to profit from short-term price movements. Stocks, currencies, futures, and options are common instruments traded by day traders. It's important to note that day trading requires active involvement in the markets and typically involves multiple trades throughout the day.

1.2 Pros and Cons of Day Trading

Day trading offers several advantages that attract individuals seeking an exciting and potentially profitable career.

Pros of Day Trading

Potential for High Returns: Day trading offers the potential for quick profits by taking advantage of intraday price movements. Skilled day traders can capitalize on short-term market fluctuations and generate substantial returns.
You

Independence and Flexibility: Day trading provides the opportunity to work independently and set your own schedule, and pursue other interests. You have the freedom to trade from anywhere with an internet connection, allowing for a flexible lifestyle.

Quick Feedback and Learning Opportunities: Day trading offers rapid feedback on trades, allowing for immediate learning opportunities. By analyzing your trades daily, you can identify patterns, refine strategies, and improve your decision-making skills.

No Overnight Exposure: Unlike swing trading or long-term investing, day trading typically involves closing out all positions by the end of the trading day. This means you don't carry the risk of overnight market movements, reducing the potential for unexpected events impacting your trades.

Cons of Day Trading

It's crucial to be aware of the challenges and risks associated with day trading:

High Risk and Volatility: Day trading involves higher levels of risk and volatility compared to other trading styles. The fast-paced nature of day trading can lead to substantial losses if trades go against you. It requires disciplined risk management to mitigate potential losses.

Time and Effort Demands: Day trading requires significant time and effort. Traders need to be fully engaged during market hours, constantly monitoring positions, analyzing charts, and executing trades. It can be mentally and physically demanding, especially for those with other commitments.

Emotional Stress: The pressure of making quick decisions and managing potential losses can cause emotional stress for day traders.

Emotions such as fear, greed, and frustration can cloud judgment and lead to impulsive decision-making.

Transaction Costs: Frequent trading can accumulate transaction costs, including commissions and fees. These costs can eat into profits, especially for traders with smaller account sizes. It's important to consider the impact of these expenses on your overall trading performance.

Market Dependency: Day trading relies heavily on market volatility and liquidity. During periods of low volatility or choppy market conditions, finding profitable opportunities can be challenging. Traders may need to adapt their strategies or even step away from the markets during unfavorable conditions.

Learning Curve: Day trading requires a solid understanding of technical analysis, risk management, and market dynamics. It takes time and effort to develop the necessary skills and knowledge.

It's essential to thoroughly understand the risks and challenges associated with day trading before diving in. Developing a solid trading plan, acquiring the necessary knowledge and skills, and practicing disciplined risk management can help mitigate potential drawbacks and increase your chances of success.

1.3 Key Day Trading Concepts

To lay the foundation for successful day trading, it's essential to grasp some fundamental concepts:

a) Volatility: Volatility refers to the price fluctuations of a financial instrument. Day traders often seek volatile stocks or assets with significant price movements, as they provide opportunities for quick profits.

b) Liquidity: Liquidity refers to the ease of buying or selling an asset without causing significant price changes. Highly liquid instruments are preferred by day traders, as they ensure efficient execution of trades.

c) *Timeframes:* Day traders focus on short-term timeframes, such as minutes, hours, or daily charts. They analyze price patterns and indicators within these timeframes to make informed trading decisions.

d) *Bid-Ask Spread:* The bid-ask spread represents the difference between the price at which buyers are willing to purchase an asset (bid) and the price at which sellers are willing to sell (ask). Traders aim to minimize the impact of spreads on their trades.

e) *Margin Trading:* Margin trading allows traders to borrow funds from their brokers to amplify their trading positions. While it can enhance potential profits, it also increases the risk of losses. Margin trading should be approached with caution and adequate risk management.

By understanding these key concepts, you'll be better prepared to navigate the exciting world of day trading. Remember, knowledge is power, and a solid understanding of the basics will serve as a strong foundation for your day trading journey.

Chapter Two

Setting Up For Success

2.1 Define Your Trading Goals

Before diving into day trading, it is crucial to define your trading goals. Understanding what you want to achieve will help shape your trading strategy and provide a clear focus. Consider the following steps:

1: Determine your motivation: Ask yourself why you want to become a day trader. Is it financial freedom, flexibility, or the thrill of the markets? Identifying your motivation will help you stay committed during challenging times.

2: Set realistic expectations: While day trading offers the potential for high returns, it is essential to set realistic expectations. Understand that trading is not a get-rich-quick scheme and that consistent profits take time and effort.

3: *Define your financial goals:* Determine the amount of money you intend to invest in your trading account and the financial milestones you aim to achieve. Establish both short-term and long-term goals to keep yourself motivated and focused.

2.2 Create a Trading Plan

A trading plan is a roadmap that outlines your approach to trading. It serves as a reference point for making informed decisions and provides structure to your trading activities. Here are practical steps to create an effective trading plan:

1: *Determine your trading style:* Identify the trading style that aligns with your personality, schedule, and risk tolerance. Common styles include scalping, day trading, swing trading, and position trading. Each style has its own time commitments and strategies.

2: *Define your trading strategy:* Develop a clear and concise trading strategy that outlines your entry and exit criteria, risk management rules, and trade management techniques. Your strategy should be based on technical analysis, fundamental analysis, or a combination of both.

3: *Set risk management guidelines:* Establish risk management rules to protect your capital. Determine your maximum risk per trade, position sizing methodology, and use of stop-loss orders to limit potential losses. Implementing risk management techniques is crucial for long-term success.

4: *Document your plan:* Write down your trading plan and keep it easily accessible. Include specific rules and guidelines for each aspect of your trading strategy. Regularly review and update your plan as your experience and market conditions evolve.

2.3 Choose the Right Brokerage Account

Selecting the right brokerage account is essential for executing trades efficiently and accessing the necessary trading tools.

Consider the following steps when choosing a brokerage account:

1: *Research reputable brokers:* Look for well-established brokers with a good reputation, competitive commission rates, and a user-friendly trading platform. Read reviews, compare features, and consider the quality of customer support.

2: *Evaluate trading platform features:* Ensure that the trading platform offered by the broker provides the necessary tools for technical analysis, order execution, and market monitoring. Demo accounts are often available for testing the platform before committing real funds.

3: *Assess commission and fee structures:* Understand the commission rates, account maintenance fees, and any additional charges associated with the broker. Compare the cost structures of different brokers to find one that aligns with your trading style and frequency.

4: Consider customer support: Prompt and reliable customer support is crucial, especially during times of technical issues or account-related queries. Look for brokers that offer responsive customer service through various channels.

2.4 Familiarize Yourself with Trading Tools and Software

To enhance your trading efficiency and effectiveness, it is essential to become familiar with trading tools and software. Follow these steps to get acquainted with the necessary tools:

1: Learn charting software: Familiarize yourself with charting software that provides real-time market data, technical indicators, and drawing tools. Popular charting platforms include TradingView, MetaTrader, and Thinkorswim.

2: Understand the Basics
Before delving into day trading tools and software, it's crucial to grasp the fundamentals

of day trading itself. Educate yourself about the key principles, strategies, and terminology commonly used in day trading. This foundation will help you better comprehend the tools and software you'll be using.

3: Research Different Tools

Day trading offers a vast array of tools and software designed to aid traders in making informed decisions. Take the time to research and explore various options available in the market. Look for tools that align with your trading goals, such as charting platforms, stock screeners, news aggregators, and real-time data feeds. Each tool serves a unique purpose, so it's important to assess their features, usability, and compatibility with your trading style.

4: Choose a Reliable Brokerage Platform

To access day trading tools and software, you'll need a reputable brokerage platform that caters specifically to active traders. Look for platforms that offer a user-friendly interface, reliable execution, competitive fees, and comprehensive customer support. Additionally, ensure that the platform integrates well with the trading tools and software you plan to use.

5: Demo Accounts and Simulators
Practice makes perfect! Many brokerage platforms offer demo accounts or simulators that allow you to trade using virtual money. Utilize these resources to familiarize yourself with the functionality of different tools and software without risking your own capital. Use the demo accounts to test various strategies, study chart patterns, and get comfortable with order types.

6: Take Advantage of Educational Resources
To maximize your understanding of day trading tools and software, tap into the vast educational resources available. Many brokerage platforms, trading communities, and reputable websites offer tutorials, webinars, and blogs that cover various tools and software. Dedicate time to absorb these resources and enhance your knowledge.

7: Start Small and Analyze Results

As you become more comfortable with day trading tools and software, it's time to start trading with real money. However, it is advisable to begin with small positions and gradually increase your capital as you gain experience and refine your strategies. Analyze your trades, review your performance, and use the available tools and software to track your progress and make data-driven decisions.

Familiarizing yourself with day trading tools and software is a vital step towards becoming a proficient trader. By understanding the basics, researching various tools, and utilizing demo accounts, you can develop the necessary skills to navigate the complexities of day trading. Remember to leverage educational resources, start small, and continually adapt your strategies.

Chapter Three

Developing a Solid Foundation

3.1 Mastering Basic Technical Analysis

Technical analysis is a key tool used by day traders to analyze market data and make informed trading decisions. It involves studying historical price and volume patterns to identify potential future price movements. Understanding the basics of technical analysis is essential for successful day trading. Let's delve into practical steps and examples:

1: Learn chart patterns: Chart patterns are formations that occur on price charts and provide valuable insights into market sentiment. Examples of chart patterns include the double top, head and shoulders, and ascending triangle. By recognizing these patterns, traders can anticipate potential price reversals or breakouts.

For instance, if you identify a double top pattern forming on a stock's chart, it suggests a potential trend reversal. This could be an opportunity to enter a short trade and profit from a subsequent downward price movement.

2: *Utilize technical indicators:* Technical indicators are mathematical calculations applied to price and volume data to generate trading signals. Examples of commonly used indicators include moving averages, relative strength index (RSI), and Bollinger Bands.

For example, a trader might use the 50-day moving average as a trend-following indicator. If the stock price crosses above the 50-day moving average, it could signal a bullish trend and an opportunity to enter a long trade.

3: *Understand support and resistance levels:* Support and resistance levels are price levels where buying or selling pressure is expected to emerge. Support acts as a floor, preventing prices from falling further, while resistance acts as a ceiling, preventing prices from rising higher.

By identifying these levels, traders can make more informed decisions. For instance, if a stock consistently bounces off a specific support level, it might present an opportunity to enter a long trade with a defined risk level.

3.2 Introduction to Candlestick Patterns

Candlestick patterns provide valuable insights into price action and market sentiment. These patterns are formed by the open, high, low, and close prices within a given time period. Here are some practical steps to understand candlestick patterns:

1: Learn common candlestick patterns: Examples of popular candlestick patterns include doji, hammer, engulfing, and shooting star. Each pattern has its own implications for market direction and potential reversals.

For instance, a doji candlestick, characterized by a small body and equal or near-equal open and close prices, suggests indecision in the market. It may indicate a potential trend reversal, especially if it forms at a support or resistance level.

2: *Combine candlestick patterns with other indicators:* Candlestick patterns are more powerful when used in conjunction with other technical indicators or chart patterns. For example, if a doji candlestick forms at a key resistance level and is followed by a bearish engulfing pattern, it could strengthen the case for a potential price reversal.

3: *Practice pattern recognition:* Enhance your ability to recognize candlestick patterns by studying historical price charts and practicing pattern identification. Use trading simulators or paper trading to gain hands-on experience without risking real money.

3.3 Using Indicators and Oscillators
3.4 Understanding Support and Resistance Levels

Practical Example:
Let's say you have a trading account with $10,000 and decide to risk 2% of your capital

on each trade. This means your maximum risk per trade is $200.

You identify a potential trade where the entry price is $50 per share. To implement proper risk management, you set a stop-loss order at $48, ensuring a $2 potential loss per share.

Now, calculate the position size to align with your risk parameters. Since your maximum risk per trade is $200, and you are risking $2 per share, you can buy 100 shares ($200 ÷ $2 = 100). This ensures that if the stop-loss is triggered, your maximum loss will be within your risk tolerance.

By implementing these risk management strategies, you protect your capital from substantial losses and preserve your ability to trade another day.

Remember, risk management is a fundamental aspect of successful day trading. It helps you maintain discipline, control emotions, and increase the likelihood of long-term profitability.

Mastering technical analysis, understanding candlestick patterns, Using Indicators and Oscillators, and Understanding Support and Resistance Levels are crucial components of day trading success. Continuously practice and refine your skills, adapt to changing market conditions, and always prioritize the preservation of your trading capital.

Chapter Four

Developing a Winning Mindset

4.1 The Importance of a Winning Mindset

Developing a winning mindset is vital for day traders as it influences decision-making, emotional control, and overall trading performance. A strong mental game can help you navigate the ups and downs of the market with confidence and resilience. Here are practical steps to cultivate a winning mindset:

Step 1: Embrace a growth mindset:
Adopt a mindset focused on continuous learning and improvement. Recognize that setbacks and losses are opportunities for growth and development. Instead of dwelling on failures, analyze them objectively and seek ways to enhance your skills and strategies.

Step 2: Cultivate discipline and patience:

Successful day traders exhibit discipline and patience in their approach. Follow your trading plan diligently, stick to your predefined rules, and avoid impulsive decisions driven by emotions. Patience is crucial when waiting for high-probability trading setups to materialize.

Step 3: Manage emotions effectively:

Emotions can cloud judgment and lead to poor decision-making. Learn to recognize and manage emotions such as fear, greed, and overconfidence. Implement techniques like deep breathing exercises, meditation, or journaling to maintain emotional balance during stressful trading situations.

Step 4: Maintain a positive mindset:

Positivity breeds resilience and the ability to bounce back from setbacks. Surround yourself with supportive individuals who share your trading goals. Focus on the lessons learned from both wins and losses, and celebrate small victories along the way.

4.2 Developing Self-Discipline

Self-discipline is a cornerstone of successful day trading. It involves the ability to follow your trading plan, stick to predefined rules, and maintain focus amidst distractions. Here are practical steps to develop self-discipline:

Step 1: Establish a routine:
Create a daily routine that includes specific times for market analysis, trade execution, and personal development. Having a structured routine helps establish good trading habits and minimizes the impact of external distractions.

Step 2: Set realistic goals:
Break down your trading goals into smaller, achievable milestones. Focus on consistent progress rather than overnight success. By setting achievable goals, you reinforce the importance of discipline and build confidence as you accomplish each milestone.

Step 3: Practice delayed gratification:
Delayed gratification is the ability to resist short-term temptations for long-term gains.

Avoid impulsive trades or chasing quick profits. Stick to your trading plan and wait for high-quality setups that align with your strategy.

Step 4: Track and analyze your performance:
Keep a trading journal to record your trades, emotions, and observations. Regularly review your journal to identify patterns, strengths, and areas for improvement. This helps reinforce discipline by holding yourself accountable and learning from past experiences.

Practical Example:
Imagine you have been following your trading plan diligently, but one day, you experience a series of consecutive losses. Emotions start to creep in, and the temptation to deviate from your plan becomes strong.

However, with a developed winning mindset and self-discipline, you recognize the importance of sticking to your predefined rules. Instead of making impulsive trades to recover losses, you take a step back, assess the situation objectively, and refer to your trading journal for guidance.

By analyzing your journal entries, you identify potential mistakes, such as entering trades that did not meet all your criteria or allowing emotions to influence your decision-making. Armed with this knowledge, you adjust your approach, reaffirm your commitment to your trading plan, and focus on the long-term profitability of your strategy.

By developing self-discipline and maintaining a winning mindset, you effectively navigate challenging trading situations and maintain consistency in your decision-making process.

Developing a winning mindset and self-discipline are critical components of successful day trading. By embracing a growth mindset, cultivating discipline, managing emotions effectively, and maintaining a positive

Chapter Five

Risk Management Strategies for Day Traders

5.1 Understanding Risk in Day Trading

Effective risk management is essential for day traders to protect their capital and achieve long-term profitability. Understanding the risks involved in day trading is crucial to develop appropriate risk management strategies. Here are practical steps to assess and manage risk:

1: Identify and quantify risk: Analyze the potential risks associated with each trade. Consider factors such as market volatility, liquidity, and news events that may impact the price of the instrument you're trading. Quantify the potential risk in terms of the maximum loss you're willing to tolerate.

2: Determine position sizing: Position sizing refers to the number of shares or contracts you trade in a given position. Calculate your position size based on your risk tolerance, the distance to your stop-loss level, and the volatility of the instrument. Ensure that your position size aligns with your predefined risk parameters.

3: Use stop-loss orders: Implementing stop-loss orders is a key risk management technique. A stop-loss order automatically exits a trade if the price reaches a predetermined level. Place your stop-loss order at a level that allows for a reasonable loss within your risk tolerance. Adjust the stop-loss level if necessary as the trade progresses.

4: Diversify your trades: Diversification is a risk management strategy that involves spreading your trades across different instruments, sectors, or markets. By diversifying, you reduce the impact of any single trade or market movement on your overall portfolio. Be cautious not to over-diversify, as it may lead to diluted focus and reduced profitability.

5.2   Risk-Reward   Ratio   and   Trade Management

The risk-reward ratio is a key concept in day trading that compares the potential profit of a trade to its potential loss. Managing trades based on a favorable risk-reward ratio can help improve overall profitability. Here are practical steps to implement effective risk-reward management:

1: Assess potential rewards: Identify the profit target or exit level for each trade. Determine a realistic target based on technical analysis, support and resistance levels, or other relevant factors. This allows you to estimate the potential reward of the trade.

2: Set risk-reward ratio parameters: Define the minimum risk-reward ratio you are comfortable with for each trade. A common rule of thumb is to aim for a minimum ratio of 1:2, where the potential reward is at least twice the potential risk. Adjust this ratio based on your risk tolerance and the market conditions.

3: Adjust position sizing:

Calculate your position size based on the risk-reward ratio and your maximum risk per trade. Ensure that your potential profit justifies the potential loss. If the risk-reward ratio is not favorable, consider passing on the trade or adjusting your profit target to achieve a better ratio.

4: Manage trades proactively: Once in a trade, actively manage it to maximize potential profits and minimize losses. Consider trailing stop-loss orders to lock in profits as the trade moves in your favor. Adjust profit targets or exit levels if new information or changing market conditions warrant a revision.

5.3 Importance of Risk Management

Effective risk management is the cornerstone of successful trading. It helps you protect your capital, minimize losses, and maintain consistency in your trading performance. In this chapter, we will explore practical steps and techniques to implement robust risk management strategies.

Step 1: Determine your risk tolerance:

Assess your risk tolerance by considering factors such as your financial situation, trading experience, and emotional resilience. This will help you establish appropriate risk parameters for your trades.

Step 2: Set a maximum risk per trade:

Define the maximum amount of capital you are willing to risk on each trade. As a general rule, it is recommended to risk no more than 1-2% of your trading capital on any single trade. This ensures that a series of losing trades does not deplete your account.

Step 3: Position sizing:

Calculate the position size based on your maximum risk per trade and the distance to your stop-loss level. By determining the appropriate position size, you can align your risk with your desired reward potential. Various position sizing methods, such as fixed fractional position sizing or percentage of equity, can be used based on your risk tolerance.

Step 4: Utilize stop-loss orders: Always use stop-loss orders to limit potential losses on each trade. Determine an appropriate stop-loss level based on technical analysis, support and resistance levels, or volatility indicators. Placing a stop-loss order ensures that you exit a trade if it moves against you beyond a predetermined point.

Step 5: Implement trailing stop orders:
Trailing stops allow you to protect profits and potentially capture larger gains as the trade moves in your favor. With a trailing stop order, the stop-loss level automatically adjusts to lock in profits as the price advances. This way, you let your profits run while still managing risk.

5.4 Avoiding Overtrading and Emotional Decision-making

Day trading can be an exhilarating venture, offering the potential for substantial profits in a short span of time. However, the road to success in day trading is not without its challenges. Two common pitfalls that traders often face are overtrading and emotional decision-making. These detrimental tendencies can lead to poor judgment, financial losses, and a lack of consistency in trading outcomes. In this article, we will explore effective strategies to help you avoid overtrading and make rational decisions, enhancing your chances of success in the dynamic world of day trading.

Understanding Overtrading:
Overtrading refers to the excessive buying and selling of securities within a short period. It is driven by the desire to be constantly in action, often resulting from a fear of missing out on potential opportunities or a compulsion to recoup losses quickly. Unfortunately, overtrading can lead to increased transaction costs, reduced focus on quality trades, and emotional exhaustion.

Set Clear Trading Goals:
Establishing clear and realistic trading goals is crucial. Define your desired profit targets and risk tolerance levels for each trade. This helps you avoid impulsive trading decisions driven

by the fear of missing out or the desire for immediate gains. Stick to your predefined strategy and remain disciplined in your approach.

Develop a Trading Plan:

A well-defined trading plan acts as your compass in the market's tumultuous sea. It outlines your entry and exit criteria, risk management strategies, and overall trading approach. By having a plan in place, you reduce the likelihood of making impulsive trades based on emotions or market noise.

Implement Risk Management:

Effective risk management is paramount in day trading. Determine your acceptable level of risk per trade, typically a percentage of your trading capital, and adhere to it consistently. Setting stop-loss orders and trailing stops can help protect your capital and minimize potential losses. Remember, preserving capital is as important as making profits.

Practice Patience and Selectivity:
Patience is a virtue in day trading. Wait for high-probability trade setups that align with your trading plan. Avoid the temptation to trade excessively due to boredom or a need for constant market action. Quality over quantity should be your guiding principle.

Emotional Decision-Making:
Emotions can cloud judgment and lead to impulsive decisions that deviate from your trading strategy. Controlling emotions is essential for making rational choices in day trading.

Be Mindful of Psychological Biases:
Acknowledge and be aware of common psychological biases that can influence your decision-making, such as confirmation bias, anchoring, and the fear of missing out (FOMO). By recognizing these biases, you can consciously counteract their effects and make more rational trading decisions.

Maintain Emotional Balance:

Managing emotions is crucial in day trading. Implement strategies such as taking breaks, meditating, or engaging in activities that help you maintain emotional balance. Avoid making impulsive decisions when you are experiencing extreme emotions, as they can impair your judgment and lead to poor outcomes.

Keep a Trading Journal:

Maintaining a trading journal allows you to reflect on your trades objectively. Document your trades, including entry and exit points, reasoning, and emotions experienced during each trade. Regularly reviewing your journal can help you identify patterns, strengths, and weaknesses, enabling continuous improvement in your decision-making process.

Overtrading and emotional decision-making are common challenges that day traders face. By implementing effective strategies, setting clear goals, developing a trading plan, and managing emotions, you can enhance your trading performance and increase the likelihood of success. Remember, day trading requires discipline, patience, and a commitment to continuous learning. By avoiding overtrading and making rational decisions, you can navigate the markets with.

Practical Example:
Let's say you are day trading a stock with an entry price of $50. Based on your analysis, you identify a profit target at $55 and determine that the stop-loss level should be set at $48 to limit potential losses.

Considering a maximum risk of $200 per trade, you calculate your position size by dividing the maximum risk by the distance to the stop-loss level ($200 ÷ ($50 - $48) = 100 shares). Therefore, you can buy 100 shares of the stock.

By applying a risk-reward ratio of 1:2, your profit target of $55 would result in a potential profit of $500 ($55 - $50 = $5 profit per share x 100 shares). This profit potential justifies the $200 risk you are willing to take.

As the trade progresses, the stock price starts to rise, reaching $53. At this point, you decide to adjust your stop-loss order to $51 to lock in some profits and reduce the risk. By doing so, you ensure a minimum profit of $200 ($51 - $50 = $1 profit per share x 100 shares) even if the trade reverses.

The stock continues to climb, reaching your profit target of $55. At this level, you exit the trade, realizing a profit of $500 ($55 - $50 = $5 profit per share x 100 shares).

By managing your trade based on a favorable risk-reward ratio, actively adjusting your stop-loss level, and taking profits at the predetermined target, you effectively mitigate risk and maximize potential returns.

Implementing sound risk management strategies is crucial for day traders. By identifying and quantifying risk, utilizing stop-loss orders, diversifying trades, and managing trades based on a favorable risk-reward ratio, you protect your capital and increase the likelihood of long-term profitability. Remember to adapt these strategies to your individual risk tolerance and continuously evaluate and refine your approach to risk management.

Another Practical Example:
Suppose you have a trading account with $50,000 and have determined that your maximum risk per trade will be 2% of your account balance, which is $1,000. You identify a stock with a potential entry at $50 and set a stop-loss level at $48.

To calculate your position size, you divide your maximum risk of $1,000 by the difference between your entry price ($50) and stop-loss level ($48). In this case, the difference is $2. Therefore, your position size would be $1,000 divided by $2, resulting in a position size of 500 shares.

By implementing a stop-loss order at $48, you limit your potential loss to $2 per share. If the trade goes in your favor and the stock price rises to $55, you could adjust your trailing stop order to $53, locking in a profit of $3 per share. This way, you protect your gains while allowing the trade to continue profiting.

It is important to remember that risk management is not limited to individual trades but should also be applied to overall portfolio management. Diversifying your trades across different instruments, sectors, or asset classes can further mitigate risk and protect your capital.

Risk management is a vital aspect of successful trading. By determining your risk tolerance, setting a maximum risk per trade, employing position sizing techniques, utilizing stop-loss orders, and implementing trailing stops, you safeguard your capital and ensure longevity in the market. Remember to consistently evaluate and adjust your risk management approach as your account balance and trading experience evolve. With a disciplined and proactive risk management strategy, you lay a solid foundation for sustainable trading success.

Chapter Six

Developing Effective Trading Strategies

6.1 The Importance of a Trading Strategy

A trading strategy is a set of rules and guidelines that define your approach to the market. Having a well-defined and tested trading strategy is crucial for consistent profitability in day trading. Here are practical steps to develop an effective trading strategy:

Step 1: Define your trading goals: Determine your financial goals and trading objectives. Are you aiming for short-term gains or long-term wealth accumulation? Clarifying your goals will help you align your trading strategy accordingly.

Step 2: Choose a trading style: Select a trading style that suits your personality, time availability, and risk tolerance. Common trading styles include trend following, breakout trading, and mean reversion. Consider the pros and cons of each style and choose the one that resonates with you.

Step 3: Identify key indicators and tools:
Determine the technical indicators, chart patterns, or other tools that align with your chosen trading style. For example, if you are a trend follower, you may rely on moving averages and trendlines. Experiment with different indicators and select the ones that provide consistent signals for your strategy.

Step 4: Develop entry and exit rules:
Define clear rules for entering and exiting trades based on your chosen indicators. For instance, your entry rule may be when the price breaks above a certain moving average, and your exit rule could be a trailing stop-loss order or a target price based on support and resistance levels.

6.2 Backtesting and Optimization

Backtesting is a crucial step in developing a trading strategy. It involves testing your strategy on historical data to assess its performance and make necessary adjustments. Here are practical steps for backtesting and optimizing your strategy:

Step 1: Gather historical data: Collect reliable historical price data for the instruments you plan to trade. This data should include relevant timeframes and indicators that align with your strategy.

Step 2: Define backtesting parameters:
Set the time period for backtesting, such as the past one or two years. Determine the frequency of trades, the position sizing rules, and any other relevant parameters.

Step 3: Execute the backtest: Apply your trading strategy to the historical data and track the performance. Take note of the number of trades, win rate, average gain/loss, and drawdowns. This analysis will help you understand the strengths and weaknesses of your strategy.

Step 4: Optimize and refine your strategy:
Identify areas for improvement based on the backtest results. Make adjustments to your entry and exit rules, position sizing, or indicators. Re-run the backtest to assess the impact of these changes. Iterate this process until you achieve satisfactory results.

Practical Example:
Suppose you have chosen a trend-following trading strategy that utilizes the 50-day and 200-day moving averages. Your entry rule is when the 50-day moving average crosses above the 200-day moving average, signaling an uptrend. Your exit rule is when the price closes below the 50-day moving average.

To backtest this strategy, you gather historical price data for a specific stock and set the backtesting parameters for the past two years. Upon executing the backtest, you find that the strategy generates a high win rate of 70% with an average gain-to-loss ratio of 2:1.

However, during the backtest, you notice that the strategy underperformed in highly volatile market conditions. To optimize the strategy, you decide to introduce a volatility filter by incorporating the Average True Range (ATR) indicator. You adjust the exit rule to include a minimum distance from the 50-day moving average based on the ATR value.

After re-running the backtest with the optimized strategy, you observe an improvement in overall performance, particularly during volatile market periods. The win rate increases to 75%, and the average gain-to-loss ratio improves to 2.5:1. These adjustments demonstrate the importance of refining and optimizing your strategy based on historical performance.

To further validate your strategy, you decide to forward-test it in a simulated trading environment or with a small live trading account. By implementing the strategy in real-time market conditions, you can assess its effectiveness and fine-tune any remaining areas of improvement.

As you gain more experience and accumulate data from live trading, you can continue to refine and adapt your strategy. Keep a trading journal to record your observations, notes on market conditions, and any adjustments you make along the way. This journal will serve as a valuable resource for continuous improvement.

Remember, developing an effective trading strategy takes time and requires a commitment to ongoing evaluation and refinement. By backtesting, optimizing, and forward-testing your strategy, you increase the likelihood of consistent profitability in your day trading endeavors.

Developing a trading strategy is essential for day traders. By defining your trading goals, selecting a suitable trading style, identifying key indicators, and establishing clear entry and exit rules, you create a solid foundation. Backtesting and optimizing your strategy based on historical data, followed by forward-testing in live market conditions, allows you to refine and improve its performance. Stay diligent in tracking and analyzing your results, and be open to adapting your strategy as market dynamics evolve.

6. 3 Selecting a Trading Style

Before diving headfirst into the exciting world of day trading, it is crucial to select a trading style that suits your personality, risk tolerance, and financial goals.

Understanding Trading Styles

When it comes to day trading, various trading styles exist, each with its unique approach and philosophy. Let's explore three popular trading styles: scalping, momentum trading, and swing trading.

Scalping: The Lightning-Fast Approach

Imagine being a cheetah on the trading floor—swift, decisive, and ready to pounce on opportunities. Scalping is a trading style that involves making multiple trades within a short span, aiming to profit from small price movements. Scalpers are known for their lightning-fast decision-making skills and ability to execute trades rapidly. This style requires discipline, focus, and a keen eye for short-term market inefficiencies. Scalpers often rely on technical indicators and real-time market data to make split-second trading decisions.

Scenario: Imagine you are a scalper sitting in front of your trading screen, monitoring the market. Suddenly, you notice a surge in trading volume for a particular stock. Using your expertise, you quickly analyze the price action and spot a potential short-term price movement. Without hesitation, you enter and exit the trade, pocketing a small profit within minutes.

Momentum Trading: Riding the Waves

If you prefer riding the waves of market momentum, momentum trading might be the ideal style for you. This approach focuses on identifying stocks that are experiencing significant price movements, driven by increased trading volume and market sentiment. Momentum traders seek to profit from the continuation of these price trends and often utilize technical analysis tools and chart patterns to make their trading decisions.

Scenario: Imagine you are a momentum trader analyzing the market. You notice that a particular stock has recently broken out of a long-term resistance level with surging trading volume. Recognizing the potential for a sustained upward trend, you initiate a buy position. As the stock continues to gather momentum, you ride the wave, gradually scaling out of your position and locking in profits along the way.

Swing Trading: Capturing the Bigger Picture

Swing trading combines elements of both short-term and long-term trading. Swing traders aim to capture price movements within a timeframe ranging from a few days to several weeks. They typically focus on identifying stocks with established trends or potential reversals and enter trades with the expectation of capturing substantial price swings. Swing trading requires patience, careful analysis of technical and fundamental factors, and the ability to adapt to changing market conditions.

Scenario: Imagine you are a swing trader scanning the market for potential setups. You come across a stock that has recently completed a corrective phase within a well-defined uptrend. You analyze various indicators and confirm that the stock's fundamentals remain strong. With conviction, you enter a swing trade, anticipating a continuation of the upward trend. Over the next few days, the stock climbs steadily, reaching your target price, and you exit the trade with a satisfying profit.

Choosing Your Trading Style

Selecting the right trading style is a personal decision that requires self-awareness and careful consideration. Here are a few key factors to help guide your decision-making process:

Personality: Assess your strengths, weaknesses, and psychological traits. Do you thrive under pressure and make quick decisions? Or do you prefer a more measured and calculated approach?

Risk Tolerance: Evaluate your comfort level with risk. Are you willing to take on higher levels of risk for the potential of greater rewards, or do you prefer a more conservative approach with lower risk?

Time Commitment. Consider the amount of time you can dedicate to day trading. Scalping requires constant monitoring and quick execution, while swing trading allows for more flexibility and fewer trades.

Market Conditions: Take into account the prevailing market conditions and your ability to adapt to them. Some trading styles may be more suitable during volatile market periods, while others may excel in calmer market environments.

Experience and Expertise: Consider your level of experience and expertise in technical analysis, chart patterns, and market indicators.

Some trading styles may require a deeper understanding of these concepts.

Financial Goals: Define your financial goals and align them with the potential returns and risks associated with each trading style. Determine whether you are looking for short-term gains or long-term wealth accumulation.

Remember, selecting a trading style is not a permanent decision. As you gain experience and refine your skills, you may choose to explore different trading styles or even create a hybrid approach that suits your unique preferences.

Selecting a trading style is a crucial step on your day trading journey. By understanding the characteristics of different trading styles, assessing your personality, risk tolerance, and financial goals, you can make an informed decision that aligns with your strengths and aspirations.

Whether you embrace the lightning-fast pace of scalping, ride the waves of momentum trading, or capture the bigger picture with swing trading, the key to success lies in discipline, continuous learning, and adapting to changing market conditions.

Remember, day trading is a challenging endeavor that requires patience, perseverance, and a solid understanding of market dynamics. By selecting the right trading style and honing your skills, you can unlock the potential for profitable opportunities and navigate the exciting world of day trading with confidence.

6.4 Identifying Market Opportunities

Day trading offers an exhilarating world of possibilities, where traders can capitalize on short-term price movements to generate profits. However, to succeed in this fast-paced environment, it is essential to identify and seize market opportunities effectively. Ee will explore strategies and techniques for identifying these opportunities, empowering you to uncover hidden gems and maximize your day trading potential. Get ready to embark on a journey of discovery and unveil the secrets to identifying market opportunities like a pro!

Technical Analysis: Unlocking Price Patterns and Trends

Technical analysis is a powerful tool used by day traders to study price patterns and trends. By analyzing historical price data and applying various indicators, traders can identify potential entry and exit points for trades. Here are two popular techniques within technical analysis:

a. Chart Patterns: Patterns such as triangles, head and shoulders, and double tops/bottoms can provide valuable insights into future price movements. For example, when a stock breaks out of a bullish triangle pattern, it suggests a potential upward trend, indicating a buying opportunity.

b. Moving Averages: Moving averages smooth out price data, allowing traders to identify the general direction of a stock's trend. The crossover of short-term and long-term moving averages can signal potential buy or sell opportunities.

Scenario: Imagine you are analyzing a stock's price chart and notice a cup and handle pattern forming—a bullish continuation pattern. Recognizing this as a potential market opportunity, you initiate a long position. As predicted, the stock breaks out of the handle, confirming the pattern and resulting in a profitable trade.

Fundamental Analysis: Digging Deeper into Market Catalysts

While technical analysis focuses on price movements, fundamental analysis delves into the underlying factors that drive a stock's value. By examining a company's financial statements, industry trends, and news events, traders can identify market opportunities based on solid fundamentals. Key elements of fundamental analysis include:

a. Earnings Reports: Strong earnings growth, positive surprises, and improving profit margins can indicate a healthy company with potential upside in its stock price.

b. *Industry Analysis:* Understanding the dynamics and trends of specific industries can reveal opportunities arising from factors like regulatory changes, technological advancements, or shifts in consumer behavior.

Scenario: Let's say you are monitoring the pharmaceutical sector, and news breaks about a breakthrough drug developed by a particular company. Recognizing the potential impact on the company's earnings and future prospects, you initiate a long position. As the market reacts positively to the news, the stock price surges, leading to a profitable trade.

Market News and Events: Riding the Waves of Volatility

News and events can create significant market movements, presenting day traders with lucrative opportunities. Staying informed about economic releases, corporate announcements, geopolitical developments, and major market events can help you anticipate market reactions and plan your trades accordingly.

a. Economic Calendar: Keeping track of economic indicators, such as GDP reports, employment data, and interest rate decisions, can provide insights into market sentiment and potential trading opportunities.

b. Earnings Season: During earnings season, companies release their financial results, often causing increased volatility in the market. Analyzing earnings reports and listening to earnings conference calls can help you identify potential trades.

Scenario: Suppose you are aware that the Federal Reserve is scheduled to announce its interest rate decision. Anticipating market volatility, you prepare by analyzing different scenarios and their potential impacts on various asset classes. As the news is released and the market reacts, you execute well-timed trades to capitalize on the resulting price movements.

Identifying market opportunities is a crucial skill for day traders seeking success in the dynamic world of day trading. By utilizing technical analysis to uncover price patterns and trends, conducting thorough fundamental analysis to evaluate company performance

6.5 Creating Entry and Exit Rules

Timing is everything in day trading, and creating effective entry and exit rules is essential for maximizing profits and minimizing risks. We will delve into the process of crafting entry and exit rules, equipping you with the knowledge and tools to make precise trading decisions. Get ready to unlock the secrets of successful entry and exit strategies and elevate your day trading game to new heights!

Establishing Entry Rules: Seizing the Right Moment

a. Technical Indicators: Utilize a combination of technical indicators to identify optimal entry points. Commonly used indicators include moving averages, relative strength index (RSI), stochastic oscillators, and Bollinger Bands. These indicators can help you gauge the strength of a trend, identify potential reversals, or spot overbought or oversold conditions.

Scenario: Imagine you are analyzing a stock using a combination of technical indicators. The stock has recently experienced a pullback and is approaching a significant support level. At the same time, the RSI indicates that the stock is oversold. Recognizing these convergence points as potential entry signals, you initiate a long position, anticipating a price reversal.

b. Price Patterns: Look for specific chart patterns that signal potential entry opportunities, such as breakouts, pullbacks, or trend reversals. Patterns like flags, triangles, or double bottoms can provide valuable indications of upcoming price movements.

Scenario: Let's say you spot a stock forming a bullish flag pattern after a strong uptrend. As the stock breaks out of the flag pattern with increasing volume, you recognize this as a potential entry signal. Taking advantage of the breakout, you enter a long position, expecting the continuation of the upward trend.

Defining Exit Rules: Securing Profits and Managing Risks

a. Profit Targets: Set specific profit targets based on your trading strategy and the characteristics of the market opportunity. Consider factors like resistance levels, previous price highs, or a predetermined percentage gain. By having a clear profit target, you can avoid greed-driven decisions and lock in gains when the price reaches your predetermined level.

Scenario: Suppose you set a profit target of 10% for a trade based on a stock's historical resistance level. As the stock reaches your target and shows signs of potential reversal, you exit the trade, securing your profit.

b. Stop Loss Orders: Implementing stop loss orders is vital for managing risks and protecting against significant losses. A stop loss order is a predetermined price level at which you automatically exit a trade to limit your downside.

Scenario: Imagine you enter a short position on a stock, anticipating a price decline. To protect yourself against adverse price movements, you set a stop loss order just above a key resistance level. If the stock breaks above that level, triggering the stop loss, you exit the trade to minimize your losses.

c. Trailing Stops: Trailing stops are dynamic stop loss orders that adjust as the price moves in your favor. They allow you to capture profits while giving the trade room to breathe in case of minor price retracements. Trailing stops are typically set at a certain percentage or dollar amount below the highest price reached after entering a trade.

Scenario: Let's say you initiate a long position on a stock, and it starts climbing steadily. To protect your profits, you set a trailing stop at 5% below the stock's highest price since entering the trade. As the stock continues to rise, the trailing stop automatically adjusts, ensuring that you lock in a portion of your gains if the price reverses.

Creating effective entry and exit rules is a fundamental aspect of successful day trading. By combining technical indicators, price patterns, profit targets, stop loss orders, and trailing stops, you can make well

Chapter Seven

Putting It All Together

7.1 The Role of Psychology in Trading

Mastering the psychology of trading is crucial for long-term success. Your mindset, emotions, and ability to manage psychological challenges greatly impact your trading decisions. In this chapter, we will explore practical steps to develop a strong psychological foundation and navigate the psychological aspects of trading.

Step 1: Cultivate discipline and patience:
Discipline and patience are vital virtues in trading. Develop a trading plan and stick to it, avoiding impulsive trades driven by fear or greed. Maintain patience in waiting for high-probability setups and avoid chasing trades that do not align with your strategy.

Step 2: Manage emotions effectively:

Emotions can significantly impact trading decisions. Learn to recognize and manage emotions such as fear, greed, and overconfidence. Implement techniques like deep breathing exercises, mindfulness, or meditation to help regulate your emotions and maintain a clear mindset.

Step 3: Embrace uncertainty and manage risk:

Trading inherently involves uncertainty, and losses are an inevitable part of the journey. Embrace the fact that not all trades will be winners. Focus on managing risk and protecting your capital rather than obsessing over individual trades. Accepting and managing losses will help you stay resilient and bounce back from setbacks.

Step 4: Develop a positive mindset:

Cultivate a positive and growth-oriented mindset. Believe in your ability to learn and improve over time. Instead of dwelling on past mistakes, focus on the lessons learned and use them to refine your trading strategy. Surround yourself with positive influences and affirmations that reinforce your confidence.

Practical Example:
Imagine you are in a trade that is not going as planned. The price starts to move against you, triggering feelings of fear and uncertainty. Instead of panicking and holding onto the trade out of hope, you remind yourself of the importance of discipline and risk management.

You take a step back, assess the situation objectively, and stick to your predetermined stop-loss level. By accepting the loss and cutting your position, you protect your capital from further potential damage. This act of discipline saves you from a larger loss and allows you to move on to the next opportunity with a clear mindset.

To manage your emotions, you implement a daily routine of meditation and visualization exercises. These practices help you stay grounded, calm, and focused on the present moment. By maintaining emotional balance, you make more rational trading decisions and avoid impulsive actions driven by emotional reactions.

Throughout your trading journey, you encounter various challenges and setbacks. Instead of viewing these as failures, you reframe them as opportunities for growth and learning. You consistently review your trades, identify areas for improvement, and make adjustments to your trading strategy. This growth-oriented mindset allows you to continuously evolve as a trader.

Mastering the psychology of trading is essential for sustained success. By cultivating discipline and patience, managing emotions effectively, embracing uncertainty, and developing a positive mindset, you lay a strong psychological foundation for your trading journey. Remember that trading is as much a mental game as it is a technical one. By nurturing your psychological well-being, you enhance your decision-making abilities and resilience in the face of challenges. Stay committed to personal growth, practice self-awareness, and consistently work on refining your mindset to unlock your full potential as a trader.

7.2 **The Role of Resilience in Day Trading**

Resilience is a critical trait for day traders as it enables them to navigate the challenges and uncertainties of the market. Building a resilient mindset helps you maintain focus, adapt to changing conditions, and bounce back from setbacks. Here are practical steps to cultivate resilience in your trading journey:

Step 1: Embrace failure as a learning opportunity:
Rather than viewing failures as setbacks, see them as valuable learning experiences. Analyze your mistakes, identify areas for improvement, and make adjustments to your trading approach. Each failure brings you closer to success if you use it as a stepping stone for growth.

Step 2: Develop a growth mindset: Adopt a growth mindset that believes in the ability to learn and improve over time. Embrace challenges, seek feedback, and persist through difficulties. Recognize that setbacks are temporary and part of the learning process.

Step 3: Practice self-care:
Taking care of your physical and mental well-being is crucial for resilience. Get enough sleep, exercise regularly, and maintain a healthy diet. Engage in activities outside of trading that bring you joy and help reduce stress. A balanced lifestyle enhances your ability to handle the ups and downs of trading.

Step 4: Build a support network: Surround
yourself with like-minded individuals who understand the challenges of day trading. Join trading communities, participate in forums, or find a mentor who can provide guidance and support. Having a support network can offer valuable insights, accountability, and encouragement during difficult times.

7.3 Developing Emotional Intelligence

Emotional intelligence is the ability to recognize and manage your own emotions and effectively understand and respond to the emotions of others. Cultivating emotional intelligence can greatly enhance your trading performance. Here are practical steps to develop emotional intelligence:

Step 1: Increase self-awareness: Pay attention to your emotions as you trade. Notice how fear, greed, or overconfidence may impact your decision-making. Take regular breaks to reflect on your emotional state and identify any patterns or triggers that affect your trading performance.

Step 2: Practice emotional regulation: Learn to manage your emotions and avoid impulsive trading decisions. Implement techniques such as deep breathing exercises, mindfulness, or journaling to help regulate your emotional responses. By staying calm and focused, you make better decisions based on logic rather than emotions.

Step 3: Develop empathy: Empathy allows you to understand and connect with others, including market participants. Put yourself in the shoes of other traders to gain insights into their motivations and behavior. This understanding can help you anticipate market movements and make more informed trading decisions.

Step 4: Communicate effectively: Effective communication is crucial in managing relationships with brokers, fellow traders, and other market participants. Practice active listening and clear articulation of your thoughts and intentions. Effective communication reduces misunderstandings and fosters positive relationships in the trading community.

Practical Example:
During a particularly volatile trading day, you experience a series of losses that start to affect your confidence and emotional state. Instead of succumbing to frustration and making impulsive trades, you remind yourself of the importance of resilience and emotional intelligence.

You take a step back from the screen, practice deep breathing exercises, and journal about your emotions and thoughts. Through self-reflection, you identify that fear of missing out (FOMO) has been driving some of your impulsive trades.

To address this, you develop a rule to pause and reassess before entering any trade that triggers FOMO. This rule helps you regain control over your emotions and make more rational trading decisions.

Additionally, you actively engage with your trading community and discuss your challenges and experiences. By sharing and receiving feedback, you gain insights from others who have faced similar situations. Their support and guidance reinforce your confidence and remind you that setbacks are a normal part of the trading journey.

Over time, you notice improvements in your resilience and emotional intelligence. Rather than dwelling on losses, you view them as opportunities to learn and refine your trading strategy. You develop a growth mindset that embraces challenges and persists through difficult market conditions.

Furthermore, you prioritize self-care by incorporating exercise and relaxation techniques into your daily routine. Taking care of your physical and mental well-being allows you to approach trading with a clear and focused mindset.

As you cultivate emotional intelligence, you become more attuned to the emotions of other market participants. This heightened awareness helps you anticipate market sentiment and make more informed trading decisions. By effectively communicating with brokers, fellow traders, and other market participants, you establish positive relationships and contribute to a supportive trading community.

Building a resilient trading mindset is vital for success in the day trading arena. By embracing failures as learning opportunities, developing a growth mindset, practicing self-care, and building a support network, you strengthen your resilience. Simultaneously, by cultivating emotional intelligence through self-awareness, emotional regulation, empathy, and effective communication, you enhance your decision-making and adaptability. Combining these qualities creates a solid foundation for long-term success and psychological well-being as a day trader. Remember, resilience and emotional intelligence are skills that can be developed and refined with practice and self-reflection.

7.4 Maintaining a Trading Journal

Day trading, with its fast-paced nature and potential for significant profits, attracts traders seeking success in the financial markets. However, achieving consistent results requires discipline, self-reflection, and continuous improvement. One invaluable tool that can significantly enhance your trading journey is maintaining a trading journal. In this article, we will explore the benefits of keeping a trading journal and provide practical insights on how to create and utilize one effectively.

Understanding the Trading Journal:

A trading journal is a personal record-keeping tool that allows you to track and analyze your trading activities. It serves as a repository of vital information about your trades, strategies, emotions, and lessons learned. By maintaining a journal, you gain valuable insights into your strengths and weaknesses as a trader, enabling you to make informed adjustments to your approach.

Benefits of Keeping a Trading Journal:

Objective Self-Analysis:

Maintaining a trading journal encourages objective self-analysis by providing a detailed account of your trades. By documenting your entry and exit points, trade rationale, and the emotions experienced during each trade, you gain a comprehensive view of your decision-making process. This allows you to identify patterns, strengths, and areas for improvement, leading to more informed and effective trading decisions.

Identifying and Correcting Mistakes:

A trading journal acts as a record of your mistakes and missteps. By reviewing past trades, you can pinpoint recurring errors, such as impulsive trading, emotional biases, or deviations from your trading plan. Armed with this information, you can take corrective actions and refine your trading strategy, ultimately reducing costly mistakes and increasing overall profitability.

Enhancing Discipline and Consistency:

Consistency is key in day trading. A trading journal helps you establish and maintain discipline by holding yourself accountable for following your predefined trading rules. It serves as a constant reminder of your trading plan, helping you avoid impulsive decisions and emotional biases. The act of recording and reviewing your trades reinforces consistency, fostering a more systematic and controlled approach to trading.

Tracking Progress and Assessing Performance:

A trading journal allows you to track your progress over time. By regularly reviewing your journal, you can assess your performance, measure your trading effectiveness, and identify areas of improvement. Tracking key performance metrics, such as win rate, average profit/loss, and risk-reward ratios, provides you with quantifiable data to evaluate your trading strategy's efficacy.

Practical Tips for Maintaining a Trading Journal:

Record Relevant Trade Details:
For each trade, document essential details such as the date and time, the traded instrument, entry and exit prices, position size, and any relevant technical or fundamental factors influencing your decision.

Include Trade Rationale:
Describe the reasoning behind each trade. Note the analysis, indicators, or patterns that influenced your entry and exit decisions. This helps you identify the effectiveness of specific

strategies and refine your approach accordingly.

Document Emotional State:
Record your emotional state during the trade. Note feelings of fear, greed, excitement, or frustration. This helps you understand the impact of emotions on your decision-making process and develop strategies to manage them effectively.

Perform Post-Trade Analysis:
After closing a trade, review and analyze its outcome. Assess whether you adhered to your trading plan, evaluate the effectiveness of your strategy, and identify areas for improvement.

Regularly Review and Reflect:
Set aside dedicated time to review your trading journal regularly. Reflect on your trades, identify patterns, and extract valuable lessons. Use this self-reflection to refine your trading strategy and continuously grow as a trader.

Maintaining a trading journal is a powerful tool for day traders seeking improved performance and consistency. By objectively analyzing your trades, identifying mistakes, enhancing discipline, and

Chapter Eight

Risk Management Techniques

8.1 Diversification and Asset Allocation

Day trading, with its potential for quick profits and high volatility, can be an exciting endeavor. However, it also carries inherent risks. To mitigate those risks and maximize opportunities, it is essential to employ effective strategies such as diversification and asset allocation. In this article, we will delve into the concepts of diversification and asset allocation, exploring how they can contribute to your success as a day trader.

Understanding Diversification:

Diversification is a risk management strategy that involves spreading investments across a range of assets or securities. The objective is to reduce the impact of any single investment on overall portfolio performance. By diversifying, day traders can potentially minimize losses caused by the underperformance of a particular asset, while benefiting from the gains of others.

The Power of Asset Allocation:
Asset allocation is the process of distributing investments among various asset classes, such as stocks, bonds, commodities, and currencies, based on an individual's risk tolerance, investment goals, and time horizon. Proper asset allocation can help traders achieve a balance between risk and reward. It is important to note that asset allocation should be regularly reviewed and adjusted to adapt to changing market conditions.

Benefits of Diversification and Asset Allocation:

Risk Reduction: Diversification helps mitigate the impact of adverse events in one asset or sector by spreading investments across different areas. Similarly, asset allocation ensures that a portfolio is not overly concentrated in a single asset class, reducing vulnerability to market volatility.

Opportunity for Growth: Diversification and asset allocation enable traders to tap into a wide range of investment opportunities. By allocating resources to different asset classes, day traders can potentially benefit from favorable market conditions and capitalize on emerging trends.

Smoother Performance: By diversifying their portfolios, day traders can aim for smoother and more consistent returns over time. This can help mitigate the effects of extreme market fluctuations and reduce emotional stress associated with highly volatile trading.

Protection against Systemic Risks: Diversification across various asset classes can help protect traders from systemic risks, such as economic downturns or industry-specific events. By not relying solely on a single sector or asset, traders are better positioned to weather unexpected market shocks.

Implementing Diversification and Asset Allocation:

Determine Risk Tolerance: Understand your risk tolerance level by assessing your financial goals, investment experience, and psychological disposition. This self-awareness will guide your decisions regarding asset allocation.

Identify Asset Classes: Research and identify the asset classes that align with your risk tolerance and investment objectives. Consider factors such as historical performance, correlation to other assets, and growth potential.

Allocate Investments: Allocate your trading capital across the selected asset classes based on your risk profile. A balanced allocation could involve spreading investments across equities, bonds, commodities, and currencies, with proportions based on your risk tolerance.

Regular Review and Rebalancing: Periodically review your portfolio's performance and make adjustments as necessary. Rebalancing involves realigning your portfolio back to the original asset allocation percentages, ensuring that your risk exposure remains within the desired range.

Diversification and asset allocation are vital tools for day traders seeking long-term success. By spreading investments across different assets and allocating resources strategically, traders can reduce risk, seize opportunities, and achieve a more consistent performance. Remember, each trader's situation is unique, so finding the right balance between diversification and asset allocation requires careful analysis and ongoing adjustments. With these strategies in place, you can navigate the dynamic world of day trading with greater confidence and potential for success.

8.2 Setting Realistic Expectations

t is crucial to approach day trading with a realistic mindset. Setting realistic expectations is not only a key factor in managing emotions but also plays a fundamental role in achieving long-term success in this fast-paced market. In this article, we will explore the importance of setting realistic expectations in day trading and provide guidance on how to establish them effectively.

Understanding the Nature of Day Trading:

Day trading involves buying and selling financial instruments within the same trading day, seeking to capitalize on short-term price movements. It requires sharp decision-making skills, technical analysis, and a disciplined approach. However, it is important to recognize that day trading is not a guaranteed path to instant riches. It demands dedication, continuous learning, and the ability to navigate through both winning and losing trades.

The Power of Realistic Expectations:

Emotional Control: Setting realistic expectations helps manage emotions such as fear and greed, which can cloud judgment and lead to impulsive decisions. By understanding that day trading entails both gains and losses, traders can approach each trade with a more objective mindset, reducing the risk of making irrational choices driven by emotions.

Avoiding Unrealistic Pressure: Unrealistic expectations can create undue pressure, causing traders to take unnecessary risks or make hasty decisions. Setting realistic goals allows for a more balanced and measured approach, reducing stress levels and promoting a healthier trading mindset.

Long-Term Sustainability: Day trading is a marathon, not a sprint. Setting realistic expectations encourages traders to focus on long-term sustainability rather than short-term gains. By recognizing that consistent profitability takes time and effort, traders can adopt a patient and disciplined approach that enhances their chances of long-term success.

Establishing Realistic Expectations

Education and Research: Invest time in understanding the dynamics of day trading, including market principles, technical analysis, and risk management strategies. Continuously educate yourself through reputable sources, books, courses, and mentorship programs. This knowledge will help you develop a realistic understanding of the challenges and opportunities inherent in day trading.

Define Your Trading Style: Recognize your strengths, weaknesses, and personal preferences when it comes to trading. Whether you prefer scalping, swing trading, or another approach, align your expectations with the trading style that suits you best. This ensures a more realistic assessment of your performance and potential returns.

Set Achievable Goals: Establish both short-term and long-term goals that are realistic and attainable. Start with small, incremental targets and gradually build upon them as you gain experience and confidence. Celebrate each milestone reached, as it reinforces positive progress and fosters a realistic perspective.

Risk Management: Implement effective risk management techniques, such as setting stop-loss orders and position sizing based on your risk tolerance. A sound risk management strategy provides a safety net, reducing the impact of potential losses and allowing for more realistic expectations in terms of profits and losses.

Track and Evaluate Performance: Keep a detailed record of your trades, including entry and exit points, reasons for the trade, and the outcome. Regularly review and evaluate your performance to identify strengths and weaknesses. This data-driven approach provides a realistic assessment of your trading strategy and progress over time.

Setting realistic expectations is a fundamental component of successful day trading. By understanding the nature of day trading, managing emotions, and adopting a patient and disciplined approach, traders can navigate the market with greater clarity and resilience. Remember, day trading requires continuous learning, adaptability, and a focus on long-term sustainability. By setting achievable goals, implementing effective risk management techniques, and tracking your performance, you lay the foundation for a realistic and fulfilling day trading journey

8.3 Capital Preservation and Position Sizing

To protect your trading capital and maximize your chances of long-term success, two critical concepts come into play: capital preservation and position sizing. In this article, we will explore the importance of capital preservation and position sizing in day trading and provide insights into how to implement these strategies effectively.

Understanding Capital Preservation

Capital preservation refers to the practice of safeguarding your trading capital and minimizing the risk of significant losses. It involves adopting strategies and techniques that protect your initial investment, allowing you to continue trading and capitalizing on profitable opportunities. Capital preservation is crucial in maintaining your trading career and avoiding potentially devastating setbacks.

The Significance of Position Sizing:
Position sizing is the process of determining the appropriate amount of capital to allocate to each trade. It involves finding the right balance between risk and potential reward, ensuring that no single trade poses a substantial threat to your overall trading capital. By effectively managing position sizes, day traders can mitigate losses and safeguard their accounts against excessive risk exposure.

Benefits of Capital Preservation and Position Sizing:

Risk Mitigation: Capital preservation and position sizing are essential for managing risk in day trading. By limiting the amount of capital allocated to any single trade, you reduce the potential impact of losses on your overall portfolio. This helps protect your trading capital from significant drawdowns and provides a safety net during unfavorable market conditions.

Consistency and Longevity: Adopting capital preservation and position sizing techniques promotes consistency and longevity in your trading career. By avoiding large losses, you can maintain a stable equity curve and avoid being forced out of the market prematurely. Consistency over time increases the likelihood of sustainable profits and overall success.

Emotional Control: *Effective* capital preservation and position sizing strategies help manage emotions, such as fear and greed, which can influence decision-making. When trades are appropriately sized and risks are well-managed, you can trade with a clearer mindset, reducing the likelihood of making impulsive or irrational decisions driven by emotions.

Implementing Capital Preservation and Position Sizing

Assess Risk Tolerance: Understand your risk tolerance by evaluating your financial situation, trading experience, and psychological resilience. This self-awareness will guide your decisions regarding the maximum amount of risk you are comfortable taking on each trade.

Determine Risk-Reward Ratio: Define a risk-reward ratio for each trade that aligns with your risk tolerance and trading strategy. A commonly used ratio is 1:2 or higher, where the potential reward is at least twice the amount of the risk. This ensures that even if some trades result in losses, the winners will outweigh them.

Position Sizing Formula: Develop a position sizing formula based on your risk tolerance, account size, and the distance from your entry to your stop-loss level. There are various position sizing methods, including fixed dollar amount, fixed percentage of equity, or using volatility-based indicators. Choose the method that suits your trading style and risk management preferences.

Regularly Monitor and Adjust: Continuously monitor your trades and assess their performance. Keep a journal to record each trade's outcome and evaluate its impact on your trading capital. Regularly review and adjust your position sizing based on your evolving risk tolerance, account balance, and market conditions.

Capital preservation and position sizing are paramount in day trading to protect your trading capital and enhance your long-term success. By employing effective strategies to manage risk and size your positions appropriately, you can mitigate losses, maintain consistency, and make rational decisions based on objective analysis. Remember, capital preservation is not only about avoiding losses but also about ensuring the longevity of your trading career.

8.4 Learning from Losses

Day trading, with its potential for rapid profits, also carries the risk of losses. While losses can be disheartening, they provide invaluable opportunities for growth and learning. Successful day traders understand that losses are an inherent part of the trading journey and leverage them to refine their strategies and improve their performance.

Analyze the Trade

After experiencing a loss, take a step back and objectively analyze the trade. Look for potential mistakes or weaknesses in your strategy, entry and exit points, risk management, or market analysis. Did you follow your plan? Did you allow emotions to influence your decisions? Identifying these factors helps you pinpoint areas for improvement.

Example: Let's say you experienced a loss on a trade where you ignored a key technical indicator that signaled a potential reversal. Upon analysis, you realize that you deviated from your plan due to impatience and a desire to chase short-term gains. This loss highlights the importance of adhering to your strategy and the consequences of disregarding key indicators.

Refine Your Strategy:

Learning from losses allows you to refine and optimize your trading strategy. Based on your analysis, make necessary adjustments to improve your entry and exit criteria, risk management techniques, or the selection of trading instruments. Continuously evolving your strategy based on past mistakes is crucial for long-term success.

Example: Your analysis reveals that you often enter trades too early, resulting in losses due to premature market reversals. To address this, you modify your strategy by waiting for additional confirmation before entering trades, reducing the risk of false signals and improving your win rate.

Strengthen Risk Management:

Losses can highlight weaknesses in your risk management practices. Review your position sizing, stop-loss placement, and risk-reward ratios to ensure they align with your risk tolerance and overall trading plan. Strengthening your risk management techniques can help protect your capital and minimize the impact of future losses.

Example: You notice that several consecutive losses have significantly depleted your trading account. On closer examination, you realize that you have been risking an excessive percentage of your capital on each trade. You revise your risk management strategy to limit your maximum risk exposure to a smaller percentage per trade, preserving your capital for future opportunities.

Embrace Emotional Discipline:
Losses can test your emotional resilience and discipline as a trader. Use setbacks as opportunities to reinforce emotional control and avoid impulsive decisions driven by fear or revenge trading. Develop strategies such as meditation, journaling, or seeking support from fellow traders to maintain a balanced and focused mindset.

Example: Following a significant loss, you experienced frustration and a strong desire to make up for the loss quickly. However, you recognized the potential dangers of revenge trading and chose to step back, refocus, and adhere to your trading plan. This emotional discipline prevents further losses and preserves your capital.

Learn Patience and Adaptability:

Losses teach the importance of patience and adaptability in day trading. Understand that not every trade will be a winner, and the market can be unpredictable. Learn to be patient for high-probability setups and be adaptable in adjusting your strategy to changing market conditions.

Example: You experienced a loss on a trade where market volatility unexpectedly increased, causing your stop-loss to be triggered. Upon reflection, you realize the need to be more cautious during periods of heightened volatility. You adapt your strategy by widening your stop-loss levels or reducing position sizes during volatile market conditions.

Learning from losses is an integral part of a day trader's journey towards success. Embrace setbacks as opportunities for growth, self-reflection, and strategy refinement.

Chapter Nine

Advanced Trading Techniques

9.1 Scalping and Day Trading Strategies

In the dynamic world of financial markets, traders employ various strategies to capitalize on short-term price movements. Two popular approaches that have gained significant attention are scalping and day trading. Both strategies aim to generate profits within a single trading day, but they differ in their methods and time frames. In this article, we will explore the concepts of scalping and day trading, their key characteristics, and how they can be effectively utilized by traders to navigate the fast-paced world of trading.

Scalping: Swift and Precise Profits
Scalping is a high-intensity trading strategy that focuses on making quick and frequent trades to capitalize on small price differentials. Scalpers aim to take advantage of temporary imbalances between supply and demand,

seeking to profit from rapid price fluctuations within seconds or minutes. Here are some key aspects of scalping:

Timeframe: Scalping operates on very short timeframes, such as tick charts or one-minute charts. This approach allows traders to swiftly enter and exit positions, reducing exposure to market volatility.

Profit Targets and Stop Losses: Scalpers typically set small profit targets, often just a few pips or cents, and employ tight stop losses to manage risk. The cumulative effect of numerous small gains can result in significant profits over time.

Market Selection: Scalpers focus on highly liquid markets, where there is ample trading activity and tight bid-ask spreads. Forex markets, major stock indices, and liquid stocks are popular choices for scalping.

Technical Analysis: Scalpers heavily rely on technical indicators and chart patterns to identify short-term trends, momentum shifts, and price reversals. Tools like moving averages, stochastic oscillators, and volume analysis aid in making quick and precise trading decisions.

Scalping and day trading are active trading strategies that require discipline, quick decision-making, and a thorough understanding of market dynamics. While scalping focuses on swift execution and exploiting short-term price discrepancies, day trading seeks to capture broader market movements within a single trading day. Both strategies can be highly profitable when executed with precision and accompanied by robust risk management techniques. However, it is essential to remember that trading involves inherent risks, and aspiring traders should dedicate time to practice, learn from experienced traders, and develop a personalized approach tailored to their trading goals.

9.2 Swing Trading and Position Trading

Within the realm of day trading, swing trading and position trading are two strategies that offer traders the opportunity to capture larger price movements over extended time periods. These approaches differ from the fast-paced nature of scalping and day trading, as they focus on identifying and capitalizing on medium to long-term trends. In this article, we will explore swing trading and position trading, their key characteristics, and how they can be effectively employed by traders seeking sustained profitability in the dynamic world of day trading.

I. Swing Trading: Riding the Waves of Price Trends
Swing trading is a strategy that aims to profit from medium-term price movements, typically lasting several days to a few weeks. It involves capturing the "swings" within an established trend, taking advantage of price retracements and subsequent continuation. Here are the key elements of swing trading:

Timeframe: Swing traders operate on longer timeframes, often using daily or four-hour charts. This allows them to identify and analyze broader market trends, distinguishing between minor fluctuations and meaningful price movements.

Trend Identification: Swing traders focus on determining the direction of the prevailing trend in the market. They use technical analysis tools like moving averages, trendlines, and chart patterns to spot potential entry and exit points. Confirmation indicators, such as the Relative Strength Index (RSI) or the Moving Average Convergence Divergence (MACD), help validate the strength of the identified trend.

Risk Management: Swing traders employ robust risk management techniques, including setting stop losses and profit targets. By managing risk effectively, they aim to preserve capital and maximize profitability over multiple trades.

Position Sizing: Position sizing is crucial in swing trading, as traders need to determine the appropriate trade size based on their risk tolerance and the potential reward. This ensures a balanced approach to risk and reward and helps maintain consistency in trading performance.

II. Position Trading: Profiting from Long-Term Trends

Position trading is a strategy that focuses on capturing long-term trends that can span several weeks to months. It involves holding positions for an extended period, taking advantage of sustained price movements. Here are the key elements of position trading:

Timeframe: Position traders operate on even longer timeframes, such as weekly or monthly charts. This allows them to identify major market trends and significant price reversals, disregarding short-term fluctuations.

Fundamental Analysis: Position traders employ a combination of fundamental analysis and technical analysis. They analyze economic indicators, company financials, news events, and market sentiment to identify potential trading opportunities. Technical analysis tools assist in pinpointing optimal entry and exit points within the broader trend.

Patience and Discipline: Position trading requires patience, as traders need to endure periods of consolidation and minor retracements. It also demands discipline to stick to the original trading plan and avoid making impulsive decisions based on short-term market fluctuations.

Risk Management and Portfolio Diversification: Position traders carefully manage risk by using appropriate position sizing, stop losses, and trailing stops. They also diversify their portfolio across different asset classes to spread risk and reduce the impact of any single trade or market event.

Swing trading and position trading offer day traders the opportunity to participate in medium to long-term trends and capture substantial price movements. While swing trading focuses on shorter-term trends within a larger trend, position trading seeks to ride sustained trends over extended periods. Both strategies require a deep understanding of technical and fundamental analysis, disciplined risk management, and the ability to identify optimal entry and exit points. As with any trading approach, practice, continuous learning, and adapting strategies to individual trading styles are essential for success. By embracing swing trading or position trading, traders can take a patient and calculated approach to

9.3 Using Advanced Order Types

Utilizing advanced order types can significantly enhance a trader's ability to execute trades with precision and efficiency. These order types go beyond the traditional market and limit orders, offering additional functionality to adapt to ever-changing market conditions and capitalize on opportunities. In this article, we will explore advanced order types commonly used in day trading, their benefits, and practical examples to demonstrate their effectiveness.

I. Stop Orders: Managing Risk and Capturing Breakouts

Stop orders are essential tools for managing risk and capturing potential breakout opportunities. Here are two common types of stop orders:

Stop Loss Orders: A stop loss order is placed below the current market price (for long positions) or above it (for short positions) to limit potential losses. It serves as an automatic exit point if the market moves against the trader's position. For example, if a trader buys a stock at $50 and sets a stop loss order at $48, the position will be automatically sold if the stock price drops to or below $48, limiting the loss to $2 per share.

Stop Limit Orders: A stop limit order combines the features of a stop order and a limit order. It includes both a stop price and a limit price. Once the stop price is reached, the order becomes a limit order, aiming to execute at the specified limit price or better. For instance, if a trader enters a stop limit order to buy a stock with a stop price of $60 and a limit price of $61, the order will be triggered if the stock price reaches $60 and will only be executed if the price is $61 or lower.

II. Trailing Stop Orders: Protecting Profits and Riding Trends

Trailing stop orders are dynamic order types that automatically adjust the stop price as the market moves in the trader's favor. They allow traders to protect profits and potentially capture larger gains during trending markets. Here are two types of trailing stop orders:

Trailing Stop Loss Orders: A trailing stop loss order moves the stop price upward for long positions or downward for short positions as the market price advances. It helps lock in profits while giving the trade room to breathe. For example, if a trader buys a stock at $50 and sets a trailing stop loss order with a trailing distance of $2, if the stock price rises to $55, the stop price will automatically adjust to $53, ensuring a minimum profit of $3 per share even if the price retraces.

Trailing Stop Limit Orders: Trailing stop limit orders combine the features of trailing stops and limit orders. They trail the market price and convert to a limit order once the specified trailing distance is reached. This order type allows traders to have more control over execution prices while still benefiting from trailing stop functionality.

III. OCO (One-Cancels-the-Other) Orders: Preparing for Breakouts or Reversals

OCO orders are designed to simultaneously place two orders but cancel one when the other is executed. They are useful for traders who anticipate breakout or reversal scenarios. Here's an example of how an OCO order can be used:

Suppose a trader is closely monitoring a stock trading at $50 and expects a significant price movement. They can place an OCO order consisting of two components:

A buy stop order at $51, triggered if the price breaks above resistance.

A sell stop order at $49, triggered if the price reverses and falls below support.

By using an OCO order, the trader is prepared to capitalize on either a breakout above $51 or a reversal below $49, ensuring they enter a trade in the anticipated direction.

Using advanced order types in day trading Using advanced order types in day trading empowers traders to execute trades with precision, manage risk effectively, and capitalize on market opportunities. Stop orders allow for predetermined exit points, limiting potential losses or capturing breakouts. Trailing stop orders enable traders to protect profits and ride trends, automatically adjusting the stop price as the market moves favorably. OCO orders provide flexibility in anticipating both breakout and reversal scenarios, ensuring readiness to enter a trade in the expected direction.

By incorporating advanced order types into their trading strategies, traders can streamline their decision-making process, reduce emotional biases, and take advantage of market dynamics in a disciplined manner. However, it is important to remember that no strategy guarantees success, and risk management should always be a priority. Traders should thoroughly understand each order type, practice using them in simulated environments, and gradually implement them in live trading with appropriate position sizing and risk controls.

Ultimately, mastering the usage of advanced order types requires experience, continuous learning, and adaptability to changing market conditions. By integrating these powerful tools into their day trading arsenal, traders can enhance their precision, efficiency, and overall trading performance

9.4 Incorporating Algorithmic Trading

Algorithmic trading has emerged as a powerful tool that enables traders to execute trades swiftly and efficiently. By leveraging complex algorithms and automated systems, algorithmic trading offers numerous advantages, including increased speed, accuracy, and the ability to capitalize on market opportunities in real-time. In this article, we will explore the concept of incorporating algorithmic trading into day trading, its benefits, and provide doable examples to illustrate its effectiveness.

I. Understanding Algorithmic Trading:

Algorithmic trading, also known as algo trading or automated trading, refers to the use of computer algorithms to execute trades based on predefined rules and strategies. These algorithms analyze market data, identify patterns, and generate trade signals, allowing for rapid and precise execution. Here are the key components of algorithmic trading:

Strategy Development: Traders develop algorithms that incorporate specific trading rules, indicators, and risk management parameters. These strategies can be based on technical analysis, fundamental analysis, or a combination of both.

Automated Execution: Once a trading strategy is defined, the algorithm automatically executes trades based on predetermined conditions, such as price levels, moving averages, or other technical indicators. This eliminates the need for manual intervention, reducing the potential for human error and enhancing efficiency.

High-Frequency Trading (HFT): High-frequency trading is a subset of algorithmic trading that aims to exploit small price differentials and market inefficiencies by executing a large number of trades in a short period. HFT relies on powerful computing systems and low-latency connections to capitalize on fleeting opportunities.

II. Benefits of Algorithmic Trading in Day Trading:

Incorporating algorithmic trading into day trading can provide several notable benefits for traders. Here are a few key advantages:

Speed and Efficiency: Algorithms can execute trades at lightning-fast speeds, reacting to market conditions in real-time. This enables traders to take advantage of short-lived price movements and capitalize on opportunities that may not be accessible through manual trading.

Elimination of Emotional Bias: Algorithmic trading removes emotional decision-making from the trading process. It strictly adheres to predefined rules and parameters, reducing the impact of fear, greed, or other psychological biases that can negatively affect trading performance.

Backtesting and Optimization: Algorithms can be backtested using historical data to assess their effectiveness and optimize their parameters. Traders can analyze past performance, make necessary adjustments, and fine-tune strategies to maximize profitability.

Diversification and Risk Management: Algorithmic trading allows for simultaneous execution of multiple strategies across different markets and asset classes. This diversification helps spread risk and can enhance overall portfolio performance.

Examples of Algorithmic Trading Strategies:
Here are a few doable examples of algorithmic trading strategies commonly employed in day trading:

Mean Reversion Strategy: This strategy aims to capitalize on price reversals after significant deviations from the mean. The algorithm identifies overbought or oversold conditions and triggers trades when prices revert to their average levels.

Breakout Strategy: This strategy focuses on identifying price breakouts above resistance or below support levels. The algorithm automatically executes trades when prices breach these key levels, aiming to capture momentum and trend continuation.

Momentum Strategy: This strategy aims to ride strong price trends by identifying stocks or assets with significant upward or downward momentum. The algorithm enters trades based on momentum indicators and seeks to capture profits during sustained price movements.

Incorporating algorithmic trading into day trading can revolutionize trading practices by leveraging technology, speed, and automation. By developing and implementing algorithmic strategies, traders can benefit from enhanced efficiency, reduced emotional biases, and the ability to capitalize on real-time market opportunities. However, it is important to note that algorithmic trading is not a guaranteed path to success. It requires careful strategy development, thorough testing, and continuous monitoring to ensure optimal performance. Traders should also consider market conditions, liquidity, and potential risks associated with algorithmic trading, such as system failures or data discrepancies.

To effectively incorporate algorithmic trading into day trading, traders should follow these essential steps:

Strategy Development: Define clear and specific trading rules, indicators, and risk management parameters for the algorithm.

Backtesting: Use historical data to test the algorithm's performance and assess its effectiveness under various market conditions.

Optimization: Fine-tune the algorithm by adjusting parameters and optimizing the strategy to improve profitability and risk management.

Real-time Monitoring: Continuously monitor the algorithm's performance and make necessary adjustments as market conditions evolve.

Risk Management: Implement robust risk management techniques, including position sizing, stop-loss orders, and portfolio diversification, to protect against potential losses.

It is also crucial for traders to stay updated with technological advancements and market trends related to algorithmic trading. By keeping abreast of new developments, traders can adapt their strategies and take advantage of emerging opportunities.

Incorporating algorithmic trading into day trading can provide significant benefits, including increased speed, efficiency, and the ability to capitalize on real-time market opportunities. However, it requires careful strategy development, rigorous testing, and continuous monitoring. By harnessing the power of algorithms and technology, traders can enhance their trading performance and potentially achieve greater consistency and profitability in the dynamic world of day trading.

Chapter Ten

Continuous Learning and Improvement

10.1 Staying Updated with Market News

In the fast-paced world of day trading, staying updated with market news is paramount to success. As a day trader, your ability to make informed decisions and adapt quickly to changing market conditions can mean the difference between profits and losses. We will explore the importance of staying updated with market news and provide you with valuable tips on how to do so effectively. So, grab your notepad and get ready to enhance your trading strategies!

Understanding the Significance of Market News:

Market news acts as a compass for day traders, guiding them through the labyrinth of financial markets. It encompasses a wide range of information, including economic indicators, corporate announcements, geopolitical events, and industry trends. By staying updated with market news, you gain valuable insights into the factors that drive price movements, allowing you to anticipate and capitalize on market shifts.

Tips for Staying Updated:

Follow Reliable News Sources:

Relying on reputable news sources is crucial when it comes to gathering accurate and timely information. Established financial news outlets such as Bloomberg, CNBC, Reuters, and Financial Times are renowned for their comprehensive coverage and analysis. Additionally, subscribing to reputable online financial platforms and utilizing market data providers can give you access to real-time news feeds, economic calendars, and expert commentary.

Utilize Technology:

Leveraging technology can significantly enhance your ability to stay updated with market news. Consider using news aggregators and RSS readers to consolidate news from various sources into a single, easily accessible platform. These tools allow you to customize your news preferences, ensuring that you receive updates on topics relevant to your trading interests.

Set Up Alerts:

In a fast-moving market, timely information is of the essence. Take advantage of customizable alerts offered by financial websites and trading platforms. These alerts can be tailored to notify you about specific stocks, market sectors, or breaking news events. By setting up alerts, you ensure that you are promptly informed of any significant developments that may impact your trading positions.

Engage in Social Media:

Social media platforms are not only for sharing memes and keeping up with friends; they have also become a valuable source of market news. Many financial professionals, analysts, and reputable news outlets maintain active profiles on platforms like Twitter and LinkedIn. By following these accounts and participating in relevant communities, you can gain access to real-time market insights, expert opinions, and breaking news.

Develop a Routine:
Staying updated with market news should be a routine part of your day trading activities. Establish a dedicated time slot in your schedule to review news updates, economic reports, and market analysis. This habit ensures that you remain informed and aware of potential market-moving events before the trading session begins. Remember, preparedness is key to success in day trading.

Staying updated with market news is an indispensable aspect of day trading. By understanding the significance of market news and employing the tips outlined in this article, you can enhance your trading strategies and make well-informed decisions. Remember, knowledge is power in the world of day trading, and staying updated with market news empowers you to seize opportunities, manage risks, and stay ahead of the competition. So, equip yourself with the right tools, stay vigilant, and watch your trading prowess soar!

10.2 Learning from Experienced Traders

To navigate the intricate world of financial markets with finesse, learning from experienced traders is essential. These seasoned professionals have traversed the ups and downs of the trading landscape, accumulating invaluable knowledge and insights along the way. In this article, we will explore the immense benefits of learning from experienced traders and provide you with practical tips on how to tap into their wisdom. So, fasten your seatbelt and get ready to uncover the secrets of successful day trading!

The Value of Learning from Experienced Traders:

Gaining Real-World Perspective:

Seasoned traders possess a wealth of real-world experience that textbooks and courses simply cannot replicate. By learning from their experiences, you gain insight into the practical aspects of day trading, such as managing emotions, developing effective strategies, and identifying potential pitfalls. Their stories, anecdotes, and lessons learned offer a unique perspective that can help you navigate the markets with greater confidence.

Accelerating Your Learning Curve:

Learning from experienced traders accelerates your learning curve significantly. Instead of reinventing the wheel, you can leverage their knowledge and expertise to avoid common mistakes and adopt proven strategies. This can save you precious time and capital that would otherwise be spent on trial and error. By learning from those who have already walked the path, you can expedite your growth as a trader.

Tips for Learning from Experienced Traders

Seek Mentorship:

One of the most effective ways to learn from experienced traders is by seeking mentorship. A mentor can provide personalized guidance, imparting their wisdom and helping you develop a solid foundation. Look for mentors who align with your trading style, have a successful track record, and are willing to share their insights. Engage in open and honest conversations, ask questions, and actively listen to their advice.

Join Trading Communities:

Participating in trading communities, both online and offline, exposes you to a diverse group of traders with varying levels of experience. Platforms such as forums, social media groups, and trading chat rooms provide opportunities to engage with experienced traders, seek advice, and share ideas. Actively contribute to discussions, ask thought-provoking questions, and soak in the collective knowledge of the community.

Attend Trading Workshops and Webinars:
Trading workshops and webinars hosted by experienced traders are excellent learning opportunities. These events often focus on specific trading strategies, risk management techniques, and market analysis. Attend these sessions to gain insights directly from successful traders, ask questions, and network with like-minded individuals. Additionally, many workshops offer hands-on exercises and case studies to reinforce your learning.

Study Trading Books and Biographies:
The trading world is rich with literature that captures the experiences and strategies of successful traders. Reading books written by renowned traders provides valuable insights into their mindset, decision-making process, and the challenges they faced. Additionally, biographies of successful traders offer inspiration and serve as a reminder that success is attainable with dedication and perseverance.

Analyze Trading Journals and Case Studies:
Many experienced traders maintain trading journals to track their trades, record their thought processes, and reflect on their decision-making. Analyzing these journals and case studies can offer valuable lessons. Look for patterns, trade setups, risk management techniques, and psychological aspects discussed within these resources. Extracting knowledge from real-life examples can be instrumental in refining your own trading approach.

Learning from experienced traders is a vital component of becoming a successful day trader. By tapping into their wisdom, you can gain real-world perspective, accelerate your learning curve, and avoid common pitfalls. Seek mentorship, engage in trading communities, attend workshops, read trading literature, and study trading journals to unlock the

10.3 Analyzing Trade Performance

Technical analysis is a powerful tool that enables day traders to analyze price patterns, identify trends, and make predictions about future market movements. In this article, we will explore the key concepts of technical analysis and provide you with practical examples of how it can be applied in day trading. So, fasten your seatbelt and get ready to dive into the fascinating world of technical analysis!

Understanding Technical Analysis:

Technical analysis involves the study of historical market data, primarily price and volume, to forecast future price movements. It is based on the belief that market trends tend to repeat themselves, and by identifying patterns and signals, traders can make more informed trading decisions. Technical analysis relies on various tools, including charts, indicators, and oscillators, to interpret market data and generate trading signals.

Practical Examples of Technical Analysis in Day Trading:

Trend Analysis:

Identifying and trading in the direction of the prevailing trend is a common strategy in day trading. Technical analysis tools such as trendlines, moving averages, and trend indicators help traders determine the overall trend in a stock or market. For example, a trader may use a simple moving average crossover strategy, where they buy when a shorter-term moving average (e.g., 50-day) crosses above a longer-term moving average (e.g., 200-day), signaling a potential uptrend. Conversely, a crossover in the opposite direction may indicate a downtrend and prompt the trader to consider short-selling opportunities.

Support and Resistance Levels:

Support and resistance levels are price levels at which a stock or market tends to encounter buying or selling pressure, respectively. These levels can be identified using chart patterns, such as horizontal support and resistance lines or trendlines. Traders often look for opportunities to enter trades near support levels or sell near resistance levels, expecting a bounce or reversal in price. For example, if a stock consistently bounces off a support level at $50, a trader may consider buying near that level, anticipating a potential price increase.

Candlestick Patterns:
Candlestick patterns provide valuable insights into market sentiment and potential trend reversals. Patterns such as doji, engulfing, and hammer can indicate shifts in supply and demand dynamics. For instance, a doji pattern, characterized by a small body and long wicks, suggests indecision in the market. If a doji forms after a strong uptrend, it may signal a potential trend reversal, prompting traders to consider selling or taking profits.

Momentum Indicators:
Momentum indicators, such as the Relative Strength Index (RSI) and Moving Average Convergence Divergence (MACD), help traders assess the strength and speed of price movements. These indicators can provide

insights into overbought or oversold conditions, which may precede a reversal or correction. For example, if the RSI indicator shows a stock is in overbought territory (above 70), it may suggest that the stock is due for a pullback, providing an opportunity for short-selling or exiting long positions.

Breakout Trading:

Breakout trading involves identifying price levels at which a stock or market breaks out of a range or a well-defined chart pattern, such as a triangle or rectangle. Traders look for increased volume and price momentum as confirmation of a breakout. For instance, if a stock has been trading in a tight range between $40 and $45, and it suddenly breaks above $45 with high volume, a trader may consider entering a long position, expecting further upward movement.

Technical analysis is a powerful tool for day traders, enabling them to interpret market data, identify trends, and make informed trading decisions

10.4 Adapting to Changing Market Conditions

Day trading is an exhilarating journey filled with opportunities and challenges. To thrive in this dynamic environment, day traders must possess the ability to adapt swiftly to changing market conditions. The financial markets are influenced by a multitude of factors, including economic indicators, geopolitical events, and investor sentiment. We will explore the importance of adapting to changing market conditions in day trading and provide you with valuable insights on how to cultivate the flexibility needed for success. So, fasten your seatbelt and get ready to unlock the secrets of adaptability in day trading!

Understanding the Significance of Adapting to Changing Market Conditions:

The financial markets are in a constant state of flux, and staying ahead of the curve requires a nimble approach. Adapting to changing market conditions is essential for several reasons:

Maximizing Opportunities:

Markets are driven by shifts in supply and demand, news events, and investor sentiment. By adapting quickly to changing conditions, day traders can seize opportunities as they arise. Being flexible allows you to capitalize on sudden price movements, breakouts, or reversals, thereby maximizing your profit potential.

Managing Risk:

Adapting to changing market conditions is not only about seizing opportunities; it also involves managing risk effectively. Markets can be unpredictable, and unforeseen events can lead to sudden volatility. By adapting your trading strategy to account for changing risk levels, you can protect your capital and minimize potential losses.

Avoiding Emotional Decision-Making:

Emotions can wreak havoc on trading decisions. When market conditions change unexpectedly, it is easy to succumb to fear or greed, leading to impulsive actions that may harm your trading performance. By cultivating adaptability, you can maintain a level-headed approach and make rational decisions based on the current market dynamics.

Tips for Adapting to Changing Market Conditions:

Stay Informed:
Keeping abreast of market news and developments is vital for adapting to changing conditions. Follow reputable financial news sources, stay updated on economic indicators, and be aware of major geopolitical events that can impact the markets. By staying informed, you can anticipate potential shifts and adjust your trading strategy accordingly.

Utilize Technical Analysis:
Technical analysis is a valuable tool for gauging market conditions and identifying trends. By analyzing price patterns, chart formations, and indicators, you can gain insights into market sentiment and adapt your trading strategy accordingly. For example, during periods of increased volatility, you may opt for shorter timeframes or adjust your risk

management parameters to account for higher potential price swings.

Be Flexible in Strategy Selection:

Different market conditions may require different trading strategies. In a trending market, trend-following strategies may be effective, while range-bound markets may require a mean-reversion approach. Being open to employing a variety of strategies allows you to adapt to the prevailing conditions and choose the most suitable approach for each situation.

Monitor Market Depth:

Market depth, also known as the order book, provides valuable information about the supply and demand levels for a particular security. By monitoring market depth, you can gauge the liquidity of the market and adapt your trading tactics accordingly. For instance, if the order book shows low liquidity, you may adjust your position sizes or consider alternative trading opportunities.

Maintain Discipline and Risk Management:
Adapting to changing market conditions does not mean abandoning discipline and risk management principles. It means adjusting your approach while still adhering to your predefined trading rules. Maintain proper risk-reward ratios, set stop-loss orders to protect your downside, and be disciplined in following your trading plan, even when faced with unexpected market changes.

Adapting to changing market conditions is a fundamental skill for successful day traders. By embracing flexibility

Part Two: A Must Do

How To Start Day Trading As A Beginner

Sure! Day trading is a trading strategy where traders aim to profit from short-term price fluctuations in financial markets. It involves buying and selling financial instruments within the same trading day, closing out all positions before the market closes. Here are some steps to help you get started with day trading:

Educate Yourself: Begin by gaining a solid understanding of the financial markets, trading instruments, and basic trading concepts. Learn about different trading strategies, technical analysis, and fundamental analysis. There are numerous books, online courses, and resources available to help you learn about day trading.

Practice with a Demo Account: Before risking real money, practice trading with a demo account. This allows you to familiarize yourself with the trading platform, test different strategies, and gain experience without financial risk. Use the demo account to refine your skills and build confidence.

Start with Sufficient Capital: Day trading requires adequate capital to absorb potential losses and support multiple trades. Consider starting with a sufficient amount of trading capital to meet the minimum requirements of your chosen market and strategy. Undercapitalization can increase the risk of being forced to exit positions prematurely or missing out on opportunities.

Define Your Goals and Risk Tolerance: Determine your financial goals and the amount of capital you're willing to risk. It's crucial to have a realistic expectation of returns and understand the potential risks involved in day trading. Assess your risk tolerance to ensure you can handle the ups and downs of volatile markets.

Select a Trading Style: Decide on a trading style that suits your personality and preferences. Some common day trading styles include scalping (taking small profits from frequent trades), momentum trading (capitalizing on strong market moves), and swing trading (holding positions for a few hours to a few days). Find a style that aligns with your goals and risk tolerance.

Choose a Reliable Brokerage

Selecting the right brokerage firm is crucial for your day trading success. Look for a reputable brokerage that offers a user-friendly trading platform, competitive commission rates, access to multiple markets, and reliable customer support. Ensure the brokerage is regulated by a recognized authority, as this provides an additional layer of security for your funds.

David wants to choose a reliable brokerage that meets his trading needs. He looks for a brokerage that offers a user-friendly trading platform, competitive commission rates, access to multiple markets, and excellent customer support. David ensures that the brokerage is regulated by a recognized authority to protect his funds.

Set Up a Trading Account: Choose a reputable online broker that offers suitable trading platforms and tools for day trading. Ensure the broker provides access to the markets and instruments you're interested in trading. Open a trading account, complete the necessary documentation, and deposit funds into your account.

Practice with Paper Trading: Most brokers offer paper trading or demo accounts that allow you to trade with virtual money. Use this feature to practice your strategies and gain experience without risking real capital. Monitor your performance, analyze your trades, and make adjustments as needed.

Develop a Trading Plan: Create a detailed trading plan that outlines your strategies, entry and exit criteria, risk management rules, and trade management guidelines. Your plan should include your target profit per trade, maximum acceptable loss, and risk-reward ratios. Stick to your plan and avoid impulsive decisions based on emotions.

Learn Technical Analysis: Technical analysis involves studying price charts and using various indicators and patterns to identify potential trade opportunities. Learn how to read charts, recognize support and resistance levels, use trend lines, and interpret common technical indicators like moving averages, oscillators, and volume analysis.

Implement Risk Management: Managing risk is crucial in day trading. Set stop-loss orders to limit potential losses on each trade. Determine the maximum amount you're willing to lose on any given trade based on your risk tolerance and account size. Additionally, consider position sizing to ensure you're not risking an excessive percentage of your capital on a single trade.

Continuously Learn and Adapt: Markets are dynamic, and it's important to stay updated on market news, economic indicators, and other factors that can impact the instruments you're trading. Learn from your trades, analyze your performance, and adapt your strategies accordingly. Stay disciplined and avoid chasing losses or becoming overconfident after a few successful trades.

Finally, we have Rachel, who recognizes that continuous learning and adaptation are crucial for long-term success. Rachel stays updated with financial news, economic indicators, and market trends. She regularly reviews her trades, analyzes her performance, and learns from both successes and failures. Rachel also seeks out online communities and forums to connect with experienced traders and gain valuable insights.

Start Small and Gradually Increase: When you're ready to start trading with real money, begin with a small position size. As you gain confidence and experience, you can gradually increase your position size. Avoid the temptation to risk too much too soon, as it can lead to significant losses.

As Marcus transitions to live trading, he starts with a small amount of capital that he can afford to lose without significant financial repercussions. Marcus understands the importance of gaining real-time experience and managing emotions effectively. As he becomes more confident and consistent in his results, he gradually increases his position sizes and capital allocation.

Focus on High-Probability Setups: Identify high-probability trade setups based on your strategy and technical analysis. Look for patterns, support and resistance levels, and other indicators that align with your trading plan. Avoid chasing trades that do not meet your criteria, as this can increase the risk of losses.

Keep Detailed Records: Maintain a trading journal to track your trades, including entry and exit points, reasons for entering the trade, and lessons learned. Analyze your trades regularly to identify patterns, strengths, and weaknesses in your trading approach. This helps you refine your strategy and improve over time.

Adapt to Market Conditions: Be flexible and adapt your strategy to changing market conditions. Different market environments require different approaches. Stay aware of market trends, volatility levels, and economic events that may impact your trades. Adjust your strategy accordingly to maximize opportunities and manage risks.

Becoming a successful day trader takes time, dedication, and continuous learning. Remember that trading involves risk, and it's important to start with a realistic understanding of the challenges ahead. This guide provides you with a solid foundation to begin your journey, but it's up to you to practice, refine your skills, and develop your unique trading approach. Always prioritize risk management and maintain a disciplined mindset. With perseverance and the right strategies, day trading can offer you the potential for financial freedom and a fulfilling career.

Remember, there are no guarantees in day trading, and success is not guaranteed. Be prepared to accept losses as part of the learning process. Always trade responsibly and consider seeking professional advice when needed.

Trading Platform

At the heart of your day trading activities lies the trading platform. It is a software application that facilitates buying and selling securities, monitoring market data, and executing trades. A good trading platform should offer a user-friendly interface, real-time data feeds, customizable charts, and a wide range of order types. Popular platforms such as MetaTrader, thinkorswim, and Interactive Brokers' Trader Workstation provide powerful tools for efficient trading.

Market Data and News Providers:
Staying informed about market trends and news is vital for day traders. Market data providers offer real-time price quotes, historical data, and other crucial information. Likewise, news providers deliver up-to-the-minute news that can impact financial markets. Trusted sources like Bloomberg Terminal, Reuters, and CNBC keep you updated with accurate and timely information, enabling you to make informed trading decisions.

Charting and Technical Analysis Tools:

Charting tools provide visual representations of price movements and patterns, helping day traders identify trends and make predictions. They offer various technical indicators, drawing tools, and chart types to analyze market behavior. User-friendly charting platforms such as TradingView, NinjaTrader, and eSignal empower traders to conduct in-depth technical analysis and develop effective trading strategies based on historical price data.

Stock Screeners:

To quickly identify potential trading opportunities, day traders often utilize stock screeners. These tools allow you to filter and sort stocks based on specific criteria such as price, volume, market capitalization, and fundamental ratios. Finviz, Trade Ideas, and StockFetcher are popular stock screeners that offer customizable scans to match your trading preferences, helping you find stocks that meet your criteria efficiently.

Algorithmic Trading Software:

Automating trading strategies is gaining popularity among day traders. Algorithmic trading software enables you to automate your trading rules and execute trades based on pre-programmed criteria. These platforms, including MetaTrader, TradeStation, and QuantConnect, provide advanced tools for backtesting and deploying algorithmic trading strategies. Embracing algorithmic trading can save time and remove emotional biases from your decision-making process.

Risk Management Tools:

Managing risk is a fundamental aspect of day trading. Risk management tools help you control potential losses and protect your trading capital. Stop-loss orders, trailing stops, and position sizing calculators are examples of tools that assist in implementing effective risk management strategies. Many trading platforms offer built-in risk management features, and standalone tools like ATR stops and position size calculators are also available to help you safeguard your investments.

Familiarizing yourself with day trading tools and software is essential for thriving in the fast-paced world of trading. By utilizing the right tools, you can enhance your trading performance, streamline your decision-making process, and increase your chances of profitability. Remember to choose tools that align with your trading style and objectives, and stay updated on the latest advancements in trading software. May your day trading journey be filled with success and fulfillment!

Techniques On Day Trading

Here are a few commonly used techniques and strategies in day trading:

Scalping: Scalping is a popular day trading technique that involves making small profits from frequent trades. Traders using this strategy aim to take advantage of small price movements by entering and exiting trades quickly. Scalpers often rely on technical indicators, such as moving averages or momentum oscillators, to identify short-term trends and make rapid trading decisions.

Momentum Trading: Momentum trading involves capitalizing on strong and sustained price movements in a given direction. Traders using this technique look for stocks or other instruments that are experiencing significant price increases or decreases with high trading volume. They aim to join the trend early and ride the momentum until signs of a reversal appear.

Breakout Trading: Breakout trading involves entering a trade when the price breaks out of a defined range or a significant level of support or resistance. Traders using this strategy monitor price consolidation patterns, such as triangles or rectangles, and wait for a breakout above or below these patterns. Breakout traders often use stop orders to enter trades once the breakout occurs.

Pullback Trading: Pullback trading, also known as retracement trading, involves entering a trade during a temporary price reversal within an established trend. Traders using this technique wait for a strong trend to develop and then look for a pullback or a retracement to a key support or resistance level. They enter the trade when the price shows signs of resuming the initial trend.

Range Trading: Range trading involves identifying price ranges in which an instrument is trading and taking advantage of the price oscillations within that range. Traders using this strategy aim to buy near the support level and sell near the resistance level. They set limit orders to enter and exit trades based on the anticipated price reversals within the range.

News Trading: News trading involves taking advantage of significant market moves resulting from the release of important news or economic data. Traders using this strategy closely follow economic calendars and news announcements to identify potential market-moving events. They enter trades quickly after the news is released, attempting to profit from the resulting volatility.

Mean Reversion Trading: Mean reversion trading is based on the assumption that prices tend to revert to their average or mean over time. Traders using this technique look for overextended price moves, either up or down, and anticipate a reversal to the mean. They enter trades in the opposite direction of the current trend, expecting the price to return to its average value.

Remember, these are just a few common day trading techniques, and it's essential to thoroughly understand and practice any strategy you choose. Each technique requires careful analysis, risk management, and adherence to your trading plan. It's also important to adapt and refine these strategies based on market conditions and your own trading experience.

What To Expect As A Beginner In Day Trading

Welcome to the exhilarating world of day trading! As a beginner, you're about to embark on a thrilling journey filled with opportunities, challenges, and the potential for financial growth. In this captivating guide, we'll explore what you can expect from day trading as a beginner and provide you with actionable tips to thrive in this dynamic realm. Get ready to unleash your trading potential!

The Learning Curve:
Imagine yourself as Alex, a beginner day trader eager to learn. Expect a thrilling learning adventure as you immerse yourself in trading strategies, technical analysis, and market dynamics. Begin by building a strong foundation of knowledge through books, online courses, and educational resources. Embrace the learning process as you explore various concepts, refining your skills along the way.

As Alex, you start by studying candlestick patterns and technical indicators. You practice identifying chart patterns and develop an understanding of support and resistance levels. Over time, your expertise grows, enabling you to make more informed trading decisions.

Emotional Intelligence:

Emotions play a significant role in day trading. Expect a roller coaster of emotions as you navigate the highs and lows of the market. Stay prepared to manage fear, greed, and excitement effectively. Develop emotional intelligence by sticking to your trading plan, exercising discipline, and maintaining a rational mindset. Embrace the challenge of mastering your emotions to become a resilient and level-headed trader.

Emily, a beginner day trader, experiences a winning streak, leading to overconfidence. However, she neglects her trading plan and starts taking impulsive trades based on emotions. As a result, she incurs substantial losses. Recognizing her mistakes, she refocuses on following her strategy and controlling her emotions, ultimately finding more consistent success.

Market Volatility:

Financial markets are characterized by volatility, presenting both opportunities and risks. Expect price fluctuations that can lead to rapid gains or losses. Adaptability is key. Stay prepared to adjust your strategies based on market conditions. Embrace volatility as a catalyst for potential profits, while also employing risk management techniques to protect your capital.

Mark, a beginner day trader, encounters a highly volatile market due to breaking news. He adapts his strategy by implementing tighter stop-loss orders and smaller position sizes to mitigate risk. By doing so, Mark successfully navigates through the volatile period, preserving his capital and capitalizing on favorable opportunities.

Risk Management:

Day trading involves inherent risks. Expect to encounter losses along your journey. However, effective risk management can minimize potential setbacks. Set realistic risk-reward ratios for each trade, implement stop-loss orders, and diversify your portfolio to mitigate risk. By maintaining discipline and managing risk prudently, you safeguard your trading capital and create a foundation for long-term success.

Sarah, a beginner day trader, carefully calculates her risk-reward ratios and sets strict stop-loss orders for every trade. She adheres to her risk management plan diligently, limiting her losses when trades move against her. Through consistent risk management practices, Sarah protects her capital and maintains a stable trading account.

Continuous Growth and Adaptation:

Day trading is a dynamic field that requires continuous growth and adaptation. Expect to invest time in expanding your knowledge, staying updated on market trends, and analyzing your trades. Engage in self-reflection, identify areas for improvement, and seek out educational resources, seminars, and mentorship programs. Embrace a growth mindset to continually refine your skills and strategies.

James, a beginner day trader, consistently reviews his trades, analyzes his performance, and identifies patterns of success and failure. He seeks out educational webinars, attends trading conferences, and actively participates in online trading communities.

Also Jacob, a beginner day trader, recognizes the importance of continuous growth. He dedicates time each day to reviewing his trades, analyzing his performance, and identifying areas for improvement. Jacob actively seeks out reputable trading forums, engages in discussions with experienced traders, and attends webinars and workshops to expand his knowledge base. By embracing a growth mindset, Jacob evolves as a trader and gains confidence in his abilities.

The Power of Discipline and Patience:
Day trading demands discipline and patience. Expect to exercise self-control, follow your trading plan meticulously, and avoid impulsive decisions. Maintain the discipline to stick to your predefined strategies and patiently wait for high-probability trade setups. By honing your discipline and exercising patience, you

position yourself for consistent profitability in the long run.

Sarah, a beginner day trader, establishes a well-defined trading plan with clear entry and exit criteria. She remains disciplined, adhering to her plan and avoiding impulsive trades driven by emotions. Even during periods of market stagnation, Sarah patiently waits for setups that align with her strategy. Her disciplined approach pays off as she consistently executes successful trades.

Building a Supportive Community:

In the world of day trading, a supportive community can significantly enhance your journey. Expect to connect with like-minded individuals through trading forums, social media groups, and local meetups. Surround yourself with experienced traders who can offer guidance, share insights, and provide encouragement during challenging times. Collaborating with a community of traders fosters a sense of camaraderie and enables you to learn from the experiences of others.

Ethan, a beginner day trader, actively participates in an online trading community where traders share ideas, strategies, and market analysis. By engaging with experienced traders, Ethan gains valuable insights and receives feedback on his trading decisions. The support and camaraderie within the community provide him with the motivation to persevere and excel in his trading journey.

As a beginner day trader, you are embarking on a captivating and rewarding journey. Expect a path filled with continuous learning, emotional challenges, market volatility, and risk management. Embrace the quest for knowledge, develop emotional resilience, adapt to market conditions, and prioritize risk management. Nurture discipline, cultivate patience, and engage with a supportive community. By embracing these elements, you unleash your potential as a day trader and open doors to extraordinary opportunities. Get ready to embrace the adventure and embark on a remarkable journey to financial success.

Congratulations and Good luck!

www.ingramcontent.com/pod-product-compliance
Lightning Source LLC
Chambersburg PA
CBHW060839220526
45466CB00003B/1165